The Mind of the Trout

A Cognitive Ecology for Biologists and Anglers

Thomas C. Grubb, Jr.

Illustrations by Rad Smith

THE UNIVERSITY OF WISCONSIN PRESS

The University of Wisconsin Press
1930 Monroe Street
Madison, Wisconsin 53711

www.wisc.edu/wisconsinpress/

3 Henrietta Street
London WC2E 8LU, England

1   3   5   4   2

Printed in the United States of America

Library of Congress Cataloging-in-Publication Data
Grubb, Thomas C., Jr.
The mind of the trout: a cognitive ecology for biologists and
anglers / Thomas C. Grubb, Jr.
p. cm.
Includes bibliographical references (p   ).
ISBN 0-299-18370-X (cloth: alk. paper)—
ISBN 0-299-18374-2 (pbk.: alk. paper)
1. Trout—Behavior. 2. Trout—Ecology. 3. Cognition in animals.
I. Title.—
QL638.S2 G885 2003
597.5'715—dc21
2002010204

The Mind of the Trout

For Jill and Mandy

Table of Contents

Preface

This book about trout thinking is intended for biologists, anglers, and others interested in the lives of trout. While some biologists focus on how natural selection has shaped trout to promote survival and reproductive success, other biologists and many anglers work to increase populations of trout in nature.

"Scientific" and "popular" publications about trout biology routinely use different writing styles. Whereas scientific articles often contain obscure terminology and long lists of references, popular articles are generally rather short on quantitative information and long on fish anecdotes. In striving to engage the attention of biologists, I have emphasized experimental research and mentioned only those descriptive or anecdotal accounts that have important implications for conceptual issues. For example, experienced anglers will surely recognize that trout do not always select food items in the manner that some theories mentioned in this book say they should. Such discrepancies between the real world and theory are important because they tell us where science has made a mistake. At the same time, to help make this book readable and entertaining to anglers and other amateur biologists, I have reduced scientific jargon to a minimum and mostly steered clear of statistics.

Angling is an important contemplative, intellectual pursuit that occupies the attention of many keen analytical minds highly trained in fields other than biology. Such abilities and training are of great potential in understanding the mind of the trout.

I thank Ralph Boerner, my department chair, for making available to me a block of time for writing.

Sara Shettleworth's important volume, *Cognition, Evolution, and Behavior,* provided the conceptual scaffold for much of this book. Ted Cavender, Terry Haines, Carl Ingling, and Joe Williams provided advice in their research specialties, while the comments of Kenneth Able and Robert Behnke improved earlier drafts. Bruce Leach and Susan Ward of my university's Biology and Pharmacy Library helped ferret out sometimes obscure references. I thank Bob Mauck and Joe Williams for many discussions about trout biology. Finally, I am indebted to the staff at the University of Wisconsin Press for championing and shepherding the manuscript, and to Jill for all sorts of things.

The Mind of the Trout

Chapter 1

A Thinking Fish

This book is about how and why trout think. A psychologist would call such mental activity cognitive behavior because it relates to how trout gather and process information and make decisions. A biologist would consider the mental abilities of trout, as well as the mental limitations of the fish, to be the product of natural selection.

Both biologists and anglers are keenly interested in what trout and their salmonid relatives—char, salmon, grayling, and whitefish—think about and why. Both scientists and fishers find that trout often mysteriously refuse to behave as predicted. We begin our excursion with a few examples of behavior mysterious to the biologist—behavior that can only have a basis in thinking.

A large body of work is called *optimal foraging theory*. Part of this theory, termed *optimal diet selection,* predicts that when a trout has the choice of eating a large calorie-rich food item, such a mayfly larva, or a small calorie-poor item, such as an emerging midge, the trout should always choose the large item. By doing so, it increases its rate of energy intake. Biologists hold that eating more leads a fish to grow faster, mature sooner, and become larger and therefore produce more offspring per lifetime. To the biologist offspring per lifetime (or, more properly, gene production per lifetime, called *fitness*) is the Holy Grail of natural selection, and it is toward fitness that a trout's characteristics, including how it thinks, should be directed.

But trout often flout optimal diet theory. According to theory, the 2-kg rainbow trout dining on midges emerging at the surface of Spruce Creek, Pennsylvania, at midday in November should show keen interest in any large mayfly imitations that they might encounter. Instead, they often reject the larger fly and are easy game for a midgesize #24 blue-wing olive. Something about the trout's thinking apparently prevents it from following the theorists' dictates.

Another example of trout that are not following theory: the fish are supposed to lead their lives in a way that helps them attain the greatest difference between the rate at which they take in energy and the rate at which they expend energy in their metabolism. Once again the underlying logic turns on the notion that the difference in energy between intake and output is available for growth and reproduction. Trout are cold-blooded, or poikilothermic, animals with body temperatures the same as the surrounding water. Therefore they should expend the least energy when in very cold water because that is when their metabolic rates are lowest. A currently influential idea is that when the food supply in a river is low, resulting in low trout energy intake, the fish should seek the coldest water they can find in which to wait for better days. In a river that is coldest at its headwaters and gradually becomes warmer downstream, this theory predicts that during intervals of low food trout should all be found in the cold headwaters. But only large trout follow this rule; smaller fish do not. Apparently, something in the mental process of the smaller fish prevents them from conforming to the rule.

Anglers have had many experiences that also suggest that their quarry are thinking. Deer-hair caddis flies are usually effective on the brown trout of Ohio's Mad River, except during a brief period around the end of March. During that week or so, when the riverbank sycamores are shedding their winged seeds by the millions onto the water surface, the fish are indifferent to the caddis lures. It would seem to be no coincidence that sycamore seeds are an almost perfect imitation of a #12 caddis, a paradoxical reversal of the usual case in which an artificial fly is intended to imitate some natural item. The trout seem to have responded mentally to the ubiquitous presence of inedible cellulose.

On certain stretches of catch-and-release water, such as Fisherman's Paradise on Spring Creek in Pennsylvania, or the stretch of North Carolina's Davidson River just upstream from the fish hatchery in Pisgah National Forest, the dozens if not hundreds of trout holding station in crystal clear water are simply not catchable most of the time. They do not respond to anything in an angler's fly box. Conversely, grayling in Emerald Lake, a glacial lake high in Montana's Gallatin

Range, will eagerly pursue almost any dry fly thrown anywhere near them. The vast difference in response between Pennsylvania trout and Montana grayling likely involves mental processes.

Dabbling a parachute Adams dry fly on the pocket water of the Middle Prong on the north side of Great Smoky Mountains National Park often produces a strike from the feisty resident rainbow trout the instant the fly hits the water. In contrast, floating the same fly down a languid pool of southern Utah's Fremont River often results in fish that drift along just below the fly for seconds on end before striking or refusing the offering. The difference between the eager Tennesseans and the epicurean Utahans would seem to be in what the fish are thinking.

Dead-drifting a bead-head pheasant-tail nymph down southwestern Pennsylvania's Yellow Creek is a usually reliable way to produce strikes. However, the day is sometimes a long one in late October when millions of maple leaves clog the stream on their way to Chesapeake Bay, and the nymph goes unmolested. Do trout lack the mental capacity to detect the fly amid the autumnal flotsam?

Fox Creek plunges toward the Snake River through Death Canyon in Grand Teton National Park. At about 3,000 m this torrent has an ether-clear pool that during a recent September held a small regiment of seven brook trout, all finning quietly into the gentle current. Around lunchtime a small piece of ham from my sandwich floated into the pool toward the fish. The first trout in line took the ham but only after it had arrived a few centimeters upstream from the fish's snout. During the next half hour the first fish took in five more bits of drifting ham, and by the time the sixth bit floated within its ken, the fish was darting more than a meter ahead to intercept it. It seems safe to assume that this trout had previously been unfamiliar with the contents of submarine sandwiches made in Jackson, Wyoming, so this change in lunchtime behavior was probably the result of its mental activity.

Fish hooked or flushed quite often head immediately to one particular underwater root mass, undercut bank, or other form of cover. This response is particularly noticeable when a fish takes a dead-drifted fly at the head of a pool and bolts back downstream to seek cover in a location that it could not see while holding its station and pointing upstream. Apparently, the trout had in its working memory the spatial relationship between itself and the cover.

All these incidents relate to mental aspects of foraging. In what follows, I will examine evidence for the existence of some of these processes. First, I consider the sensory systems and other factors internal to a trout that determine the information that reaches its brain. Then I turn to a trout's perceptive abilities and to what influences how well a fish pays attention to aspects of its stream. Then I will address mechanisms of learning and memory and conclude with what we know of the decision-making process. Many of these topics have been more extensively investigated in other vertebrates, particularly birds and mammals, but some work with trout and other fish species does exist. For lack of information on salmonid fishes, the trout and their relatives, I will not treat independently such topics as timing, counting, and rate determination, which have been studied intensively in higher animals, particularly birds and mammals.

An interesting line to pursue will be questions about why the mental processes of trout might not be as impressive as, say, those of chimpanzees or humans. Given the costs and benefits related to reproduction, why can trout smell better than we can but not remember things as well? Throughout the book I will point out opportunities for study of trout thinking processes. Appendix 1 details how the inquisitive angler might carry out such studies.

Chapter 2

Sensory Systems for Monitoring External Stimuli

The trout's sensory systems provide it with information about its external and internal environments. This information, both new and from past experience, forms the basis of a trout's mental processes.

I should note that I will address how hormones influence a trout's central nervous system. Hormones are chemicals that are secreted into the bloodstream by specialized glands and are carried in the plasma to all parts of the body. Individual hormones influence the function of various organs at remote sites in the body and together have a profound effect on the biology of trout. Boney fishes such as trout and salmon have eleven glands, called endocrine glands, each of which secretes one or more hormones into the bloodstream (Bone et al. 1995). Rather than present a pedestrian list of these glands and their products, I will discuss only those hormones relevant to a trout's perception of specific external or internal stimuli.

Vision

Because trout find food predominantly by sight, let me begin by discussing the physical attributes of light under water (Loew and McFarland 1990). Then we will look closely at the characteristics of the trout's eye to determine what sort of information about the world it can send to the brain.

Before it enters water, light from the sun (or moon or stars) is attenuated by the earth's atmosphere, with the degree of attenuation directly related to the length of its path and inversely related to its wavelength. Winter and blue light are attenuated more than summer and red light. At an air-water boundary some solar radiation is absorbed, some is reflected, and some is transmitted. The extent to which each of these three processes occurs is a function of the angle at which the beam hits the surface and the diffractive index of water (Dull et al. 1960).

The angle at which light enters water is of great importance to trout because it influences their ability to detect prey and predators both above and below the water's surface. Because water is a much denser medium than air, when light moves from air into water, it slows down. Because of this abrupt change in speed, when an airborne beam of light enters water at any angle other than 90° to the water's surface, it undergoes an abrupt change in direction: it bends. This bending is called *diffraction* and occurs whenever light moves between media in which it progresses at different speeds.

Anglers are familiar with a phenomenon that physicists call *Snell's Window,* namely, the size of the circular area of the water's surface through which fish can view images transmitted from above. Beyond the "rooftop" area of Snell's Window, a trout can see only reflected images from its underwater surroundings. Because light slows as it enters water, when we look at a trout under water, it appears to be farther away than it really is, and when a trout views us through Snell's Window, we appear closer than we really are. Anglers stalking trout in clear streams may wish to keep this asymmetry in mind.

The critical angle of Snell's Window is 48.5°. If the light angle in water exceeds the critical angle, light from air will be entirely reflected by the air-water boundary; the trout will not detect the light. That is, any light coming from the air that would move through water at more than 48.5° from the vertical will not enter the water at all but will be entirely reflected, and the trout will not see the angler.

At least two properties of the critical angle are of particular interest. The first stems from its being an angle, rather than any particular distance. Therefore, the farther below the surface a trout is holding, the larger Snell's Window will be and the farther you (or a predator such as a heron) must be from the fish to avoid being detected. Second, because the area beyond Snell's Window reflects images from underwater, a fish may use such reflections to see past obstructions to direct vision such as rocks and logs. We might use such an ability to sneak up on prey. Might trout do so with, say, a crayfish?

In pure water blue light (a wavelength of about 460 nanometers [nm]) transmits best, with attenuation increasing for both shorter and longer wavelengths. However, the rate of attenuation in pure water is very low, so such clear water begins to appear blue only when the path length of the view is long.

It now appears that trout can detect ultraviolet (UV—320 to 390 nm) and polarized light, both abilities that humans do not have. Loew and McFarland (1990) have suggested that fish may be able to detect UV radiation as deep as 100 m in the clear ocean.

Before we consider how trout might use the detection of polarized light to their advantage, let us review the characteristics of polarized light in water. Polarized light consists of light waves vibrating in only one plane. Solar light is unpolarized when it reaches the outermost veil of the earth's atmosphere. By the time it reaches the earth's surface, such light has become highly polarized. Polarization is greatest in the plane of a circle perpendicular to the angle at which solar radiation strikes the earth. Therefore, on the equator at solar noon of the spring or fall equinox the plane of maximum polarization will be parallel to the horizon. At sunset maximum polarization is in a plane perpendicular to the earth's surface. When viewed through polarizing sunglasses, polarization appears as an arc of darker-than-normal sky that extends in an arc perpendicular to a line between the sun and an observer when the sun is behind the observer.

Polarization is maximal for light that is moving in one direction. Any factor that disrupts this movement will reduce the extent of polarization. Therefore both turbidity and cloud cover (which can be thought of as atmospheric turbidity) reduce the polarization of light in water. Aside from the suspension of particulate matter, turbidity increases with the density of plankton. Therefore we might expect fish in clear water to have the most well-developed responses to polarization.

The Eye

In its general construction the eye of a trout follows the camera-like plan of the vertebrate eye. Incoming light passes through the cornea, is focused by a lens, and projects an upside-down and backward image on the retina at the back of the eye. Several interesting and unique features of fish eyes are associated with their aqueous environment. The refractive indexes of the cornea and ocular fluids are similar to that of water because they have similar densities, so the refraction of light required to focus an image occurs primarily in the lens (Bone et al. 1995). The fish lens is nearly spherical, a shape that gives it greater ability to refract light than the lens-shaped lens of the terrestrial eye. Thanks to the spherical shape of its lens, the fish's eye focuses all parts of the image at the same distance, a requirement for acute vision (Fernald 1990).

Accommodation is the ability to focus images coming to the eye from different distances in the environment. For example, the trout's eye can focus on a mayfly dun 5 cm away as well as on a mink swimming 5 m away. Accommodation occurs through changes in shape or position of the lens. Within the eye of land vertebrates, the contraction of ocular muscles changes the shape of the lens to make it thicker or thinner, thereby allowing the animal to focus clearly on images at different distances. Perhaps because the composition and spherical shape of the trout lens make it too dense and bulky to be thinned or thickened by muscular contraction, the trout eye accommodates by having ocular muscles move the entire lens back and forth parallel to the plane of the pupil. Such movement shifts the image to areas of the retina closer to or farther away from the lens, thus preserving a sharp image (Fernald 1990).

In its underwater environment what does a trout actually see? Visual perceptions, along with many other forms of environmental and internal stimuli, determine the fish's behavioral responses to something it sees. R. H. Douglas and C. W. Hawryshyn (1990) have developed a number of techniques for measuring perception that involve both innate (i.e., unlearned) responses and learned behavior to determine the limits of trout's visual capabilities.

The range of light intensities over 24 hours is enormous. Trout and most other vertebrates cope with this variation by using a two-stage receptor system, the rods and cones. The primary function of rods is to capture and transmit information about light at low levels. This is accomplished by sacrificing visual acuity and the ability to perceive colors. At higher light levels, where detection of light is no longer of paramount importance, the cone system comes into play to provide color vision and increased acuity.

Perhaps the most fundamental measure of visual capability is absolute sensitivity, the minimum amount of light to which an animal will respond behaviorally. We have no direct tests of absolute sensitivity in salmonids (trout and their relatives), but goldfish can respond to light intensities only 15% as bright as the minimum detectable by humans. It is not surprising, given the attenuating power of water, that fish can see in dim conditions. The development of rods lags behind the growth of cones in the eyes of young fish. Several studies have found behavioral evidence for this lag, with absolute sensitivity increasing during larval development.

Unlike terrestrial vertebrates, trout and other fishes cannot change the diameter of their pupil. Thus they have no means to control the amount of light entering the eye. Because they cannot protect the extremely light-sensitive rods by narrowing the opening of the pupil, fish have evolved a different method of protection. It involves moving the light-sensitive component of each rod into a masking pigment within the retina. This process takes 20 to 30 minutes at dusk, and its reversal takes a similar amount of time at dawn (Bone et al. 1995).

Because the eye continues to grow along with the rest of the trout during its lifetime, we might imagine that the problem of sensitivity to bright light might become increasingly severe for large old fish as the diameter of the pupil continues to enlarge. However, because the distance between the pupil opening and the retina also increases as the eye grows, and because light intensity falls off exponentially with distance, the light per unit area of retina in fact remains rather constant (Fernald 1990).

Once a fish has sufficient light to see, a second important capability involves brightness or contrast discrimination. For example, the ability to perceive prey depends on the ability to detect a contrast between its brightness and the brightness of the background. The usual method for assessing contrast discrimination is to determine the minimum percentage difference between brightness of an object and the brightness of the background. An important generalization is that the ability of fish to detect a contrast between object and background decreases as the the background becomes darker. The implications for feeding trout are made clear by the demonstration that bluegill sunfish reacted to more distant prey under higher light levels (Vinyard and O'Brien 1976). Various salmonids differ in their ability to detect prey in low light intensities. In an Arizona study (Robinson and Tash 1979) brown trout were able to detect and capture food items in experimental light intensities down to those mimicking starlight, about 0.0001 of a foot-candle, whereas Apache trout could only do so down to light intensities characteristic of moonlit nights, 0.01 of a foot-candle. That is, brown trout could see to feed in light intensities a hundred times dimmer than Apache trout could. This difference in sensitivity may explain why, in the Arizona streams where native Apache trout and introduced brown trout may both be found, the former is much more likely to be away from cover and active during the day.

Given adequate light, what is the visual acuity of a trout, its ability to discriminate the small details of an object? A common measurement of acuity is the smallest angle between two objects, calibrated in minutes of arc (1 minute of arc = 1/60 of a degree = 1/21,600 of the circumference of a circle). In other words, the smaller the angle, the more acute the vision. Rahmann and colleagues (1979) have shown that rainbow trout can detect the presence of more than one object if the angle between those objects is at least 14.0 minutes of arc. Albacore tuna were the champions in one compilation—they could detect two objects separated by only 3.7 minutes of arc. In humans the minimum separable angle is about 1 minute of arc, more acute than any known fish species. As with contrast discrimination, visual acuity increases with ambient light intensity. Trout can detect smaller objects in brighter conditions.

Acuity is directly related to the density of cone cells in the retina in a way that is exactly analogous to the tenfold increase in pixel density of high-resolution television compared to that of conventional television. Stream-dwelling trout are drift feeders and appear to devote most of their visual attention to the front and above. Keeping in mind that the image on the retina is upside down and backward, we might expect cone density to be greatest in the lower rear quarter of the retinal surface. Such an arrangement seems to be the case in rainbow trout and across several species of salmon in which densities greater than 6,000 cones per mm² tended to occur mostly on the lower and rear margins of the retina (Beaudet et al. 1997).

Fish have indeterminate growth, which means that they continue to gain size throughout their lives, although typically the rate of growth decreases with age. Such a growth pattern means that the eye continues to enlarge as well. What is the effect on acuity? It turns out that any decrease in density of cone cells on the retina that might be caused by increased retinal area is more than compensated for by the addition of new cone cells. The result is that acuity increases with fish size. Larger (and usually older) trout can see prey farther away than young fish can. Later, we will explore the consequences of age-related acuity for diet selection and within-species competition.

Trout have good color vision. For example, a rainbow trout's eyes contain different types of cone cells that are most sensitive to wavelengths of light of about 580 nm (red), 530 nm (green) or 440 nm (blue) (see figure 2.1). Jacobs (1992) and Hawryshyn and Hárosi (1994) have verified that trout and other salmonid species also possess a unique cone cell that is sensitive to wavelengths shorter than 400 nm, the part of the ultraviolet spectrum that humans cannot see. Within the ultraviolet range, rainbow trout are most sensitive to wavelengths of about 370 nm (Hawryshyn and Hárosi 1994) and brown trout to somewhat shorter wavelengths of about 355 nm (Jacobs 1992). Because water absorbs and scatters ultraviolet wavelengths to a greater extent than longer wavelengths, these cone cells may aid in some function of vision other than contrast discrimination. However, a fair amount of UV radiation penetrates at least shallow water, and it has been proposed that in such shallows, detection of UV could aid a fish in contrast discrimination of food sources. When they are still quite small, trout feed on daphnia and other small invertebrate animals collectively termed *zooplankton*. Browman and colleagues (1994) found that in full-spectrum light young fish pursued daphnia at somewhat greater distances than in light from which UV wavelengths had been removed by filters. Such an important function of UV cones for feeding in young trout was buttressed by the apparent loss of such cones as the fish aged (Bowmaker and Kunz 1987) and left shallow water habitats for depths sufficient to block UV radiation. However, Hawryshyn and McFarland (1987) found that UV cones never completely disappear from the retina but

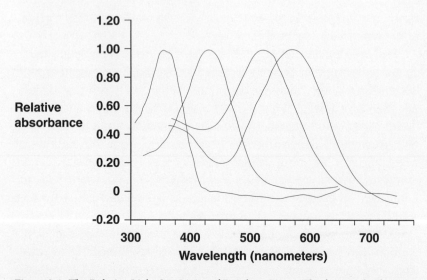

Figure 2.1. The Relative Light Sensitivity of Rainbow Trout. The four peaks denoting great sensitivity correspond to the four types of cone cells in the eye. Researchers have recently determined that trout are very sensitive to ultraviolet (UV) light. UV sensitivity is shown here by the high values of relative absorbance at wavelengths of about 370 nm. A nanometer is one billionth of a meter. (After Hawryshyn and Hárosi 1994)

continue to be produced at low rates and quickly die. Such short-lived cells are the rule through much of a fish's life. At sexual maturity the UV cones no longer die but instead build up in density within the retina. In mature chinook, coho, and chum salmon, and in rainbow trout, such UV-sensitive cones are concentrated in the rear half of the retina.

Salmon as large as 30 kg are not interested in eating plankton, so what other function might detection of UV light serve? One line of evidence suggests that UV cones are involved in the detection of polarized light, which in turn could be involved in mechanisms of celestial navigation during migration (Hawryshyn and McFarland 1987).

The direction of vibration of the light-wave form in polarized light is called the *e-vector*. UV cones in the eye preferentially detect e-vectors vibrating at right angles to the e-vectors detected by red or green cones. Presumably, this difference occurs because each UV cone has its own tiny polarizing filter, and all polarizing filters in UV cones are oriented in the same direction. The same arrangement would apply to red and green cones, except that those cones would have their polarizing filters oriented at right angles to the filters in UV cones. The direction of any e-vector in the environment, then, could be determined if the trout's central nervous system were to compare the extent of stimulation of the UV versus red and green cones.

Rainbow trout can detect and respond to the plane of polarized light. In a behavioral study (Hawryshyn et al. 1990) young (30 to 40 g) hatchery-raised fish in different treatment groups learned to seek refuge in a circular tank when the plane of polarized light was either parallel or perpendicular to the long axis of their body. The pineal organ is an extension of the brain located just beneath the roof of the skull and sensitive to light intensity (Bone et al. 1995). An opaque patch placed over the pineal organ did not abolish the response, which indicates that a receptor in the eye is responsible for the behavior. Older fish (50 to 60 g) no longer responded to polarization, which is consistent with their loss of UV cones. From more recent work it now appears that through retention of newly produced UV cones, salmon and trout may regain sensitivity to polarized light at maturity (Beaudet et al. 1997). Therefore, it will be worthwhile to pursue the possibility that navigation in oceans and large lakes involves responses to the plane of polarized light. In particular, if salmonids use a compass mechanism based on the position of the sun to find their way in large bodies of water without useful landmarks, they might use detection of polarized light to find the sun's position when clouds obscure it. Such polarized sightings of the sun might be most effective at dawn and dusk when the highest degree of polarization is directly overhead (Horvath and Varju 1995).

Now that we know that some salmonids refresh the supply of UV-sensitive cones in their eyes at maturity, it will be worthwhile to determine how far this characteristic extends within the group. If UV cones at maturity are indeed associated with sun-compass navigation in the high seas or Great Lakes, has the characteristic been lost in Gila trout, a species that remains stream-bound throughout life? Are coaster brook trout better endowed with UV cones than stream-dwelling forms?

Many questions remain about this newly discovered resurgence of UV cones in mature salmonids. For example, it is not uncommon in November to have a 30-cm male brown trout express milt (semen) when held in the hand. Such a fish is, by definition, sexually mature. What is the nature of its UV cones? If such a fish and, by implication, all larger members of the same species, can see UV light, what is the reflectance in the UV of their food items? Those fly tiers endeavoring to match the appearance of hatches might find the answer to the latter question of considerable interest.

Mechanical Perception

Mechanical perception is sensitivity to vibrations within water. Although probably not as important as vision for detecting prey, mechanical perception by the ear and lateral line organ certainly is a method that trout use to find their food. Detection of vibrations also helps trout perceive and evaluate water currents and probably to detect approaching predators. Before we turn to how trout detect vibrations, reviewing certain properties of underwater sound will be useful (Hawkins 1993).

Sound results from mechanical disturbance of a medium. As an object vibrates in water, it generates a traveling wave in which particles of the medium are alternately forced together and apart. Thus sound production involves the small reciprocating longitudinal movement of particles, which creates pressure waves (on the order of nanometers) without any net displacement of individual water molecules. Water has a greater density and higher speed of sound travel than air and is therefore a good medium for propagating sound.

All animals produce sound pressure waves when moving in water, and fish can detect these waves. Sound travels quickly in water, five times faster than in air, so water provides early warning of the approach of a predator or prey. (In water sound moves at the rate of 1,450 m per second, or 3,190 mph.) Sounds of low frequency, which have long wavelengths, "bend" around objects such as boulders that would block the much shorter wavelengths of light.

Fish have two principal structures for detecting sound vibrations, the inner ear and the lateral line organ (Schellart and Wubbels 1998). The functioning of both structures depends on a displacement detector, the hair cell. The main operational components of the inner ear are the three otolith organs, oriented at right angles to each other. Each otolith is essentially a small particle of calcium carbonate that is floating in a confined fluid-filled space. On the wall of this cavity is a structure called the *maculum,* which consists of a layer of hair cells protruding into the space. Because a fish's body is about the same density as the surrounding water, sound vibrations move essentially unchanged from the water on through the fish. However, because an otolith is much more dense than the fish and because it is suspended in fluid, the otolith lags behind the rest of the fish in responding to incoming vibration. As it lags, the otolith deflects hairs on the surrounding hair cells; when this happens, the cells send an electrical impulse to the brain (Schellart and Wubbels 1998).

A second way that sound stimulates the hair cells of the inner ear is through the action of the swim bladder. The swim bladder, also useful in controlling buoyancy, and in producing sound in some fishes, has a boundary membrane, or wall, that oscillates in response to incoming sound. When transmitted through the fish's body to the hair cells of the inner ear, swim bladder oscillations also cause impulses associated with sound detection to be sent to the brain.

Considering the role that hearing could play in the thinking and behavior of trout, two auditory abilities are of interest: how faint a sound a trout can hear, and how well a trout can pinpoint the direction of the origin of a sound. Tested at a range of sound frequencies from 30 to 400 Hz (i.e., 30 to 400 cycles per second), Atlantic salmon are most sensitive at about 175 Hz, becoming more hard of hearing as sound frequencies become either lower or higher (Hawkins and Johnstone 1973) (see figure 2.2). Although humans can hear frequencies exceeding 15 kHz (15,000 cycles per second), most fish are deaf to sounds above 2 or 3 kHz. The lower limit of hearing in fish is less well known, but Knudsen and colleagues (1997) found that juvenile chinook salmon and rainbow trout fled in response to artificially generated sounds of 10 Hz, a response that was quite resistant to behavioral extinction, suggesting it has adaptive value. We call 10 Hz *infrasound* because it is too low for our inner ears to detect. Thus we add infrasound to polarized and UV light as phenomena detectable by trout but not by us.

Salmon are harder of hearing at any frequency than are either cod or a species of freshwater catfish (Hawkins 1993). The sensitivity of the

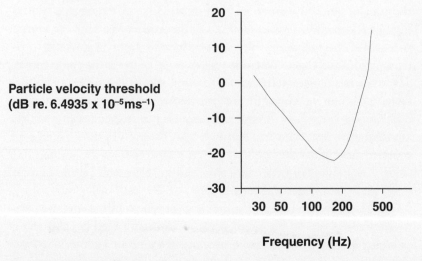

Particle velocity threshold
(dB re. 6.4935 x 10⁻⁵ms⁻¹)

Figure 2.2. Minimum Sound Levels Detectable by Atlantic Salmon. The audiogram shows that salmon were most sensitive to sound frequencies of about 175 Hz, the lowest point on the curve. A hertz is a cycle per second. (After Hawkins and Johnstone 1978)

trout ear is, however, also a function of background noise. Research with ocean-going salmon has shown that their hearing ability decreases dramatically as the level of background noise from wave clutter increases (Hawkins and Johnstone 1973). We might expect a similar result in stream-dwelling fish, depending on whether they are holding in a pool or a riffle. Night angling with a deer-hair mouse might be most successful in quiet pools.

Terrestrial animals use the difference in the time that a sound arrives at the two ears to pinpoint the source of that sound. While we have some evidence that the time lag in sound arrival is also a relevant cue in fish (Moulton and Dixon 1967), other possibilities exist. Because the hair cells of the three macula are oriented at right angles to each other, vector analysis in the brain of electrical impulse traffic from these three groups of receptors in the same ear could allow a fish to determine the direction of an incoming sound. Some evidence exists that trout and other fish may gather more precise information about sound direction by comparing the hair cell responses in the two ears to a combination of direct vibrations coming through the body and indirect vibrations coming through the swim bladder. Although no experimental evidence exists for trout, Bulwalda and colleagues (1983) have shown that cod can determine the direction of a sound source to within 10 or 20° and to discriminate between sound sources at different distances (Schuijf and Hawkins 1983). Bear in mind that cod live in the relative quiet of the deep open ocean, whereas stream-dwelling trout must contend with high levels of ambient noise that may prevent such fine discrimination of direction and distance by sound.

The lateral line and associated mast cells make up the second system by which trout sense vibrations in the environment. The basic plan of the lateral line in adult fish consists of a series of canals just under the body surface on each side of the fish, one extending over the eye, one under the eye, one out along the lower jaw, and one back along the flank. Within the canals of the lateral line are a series of neuromast organs, essentially miniature macula containing hair cells sensitive to deflection by mechanical pressure. Free neuromasts, with their own hair cells, also occur over much of the body surface. The arrangement of the hair cells in each neuromast of the lateral line is such that they are most sensitive to displacement along the axis of the canal. Such an arrangement produces a long string, or baseline, of mechanical receptors, and much of the use of the lateral line involves comparing pressure responses along its length. Pressure is transmitted from the environment to the hair cells of the neuromasts through pores in the canals, and the pores may actually extend through the overlying scales. Neuromasts free on the body surface tend to detect velocity of the water medium, while neuromasts housed within the lateral line are more attuned to the change in velocity (that is, the acceleration) of the water medium with time. Both are extremely sensitive indicators, with free neuromasts detecting water movement of less than 0.03 mm per second (0.000066 mph) and canal neuromasts sensitive to fluid acceleration of 0.3 to 20 mm per second per second (0.00066 to 0.044 mph per hour) (Bleckmann 1993).

Not surprisingly, a nerve connects each hair cell of each neuromast to the central nervous system. Nerves sending messages from the body to the brain are called *afferent nerves*. What is intriguing about neuromasts is that they also receive messages from the brain through what are termed *efferent nerves*. Thus commands from the brain apparently can adjust the sensitivity of the lateral line organs. One use of this control might be to inhibit the sensitivity of the hair cells during powerful thrusts of the trunk and tail during accelerated bursts of swimming.

How does the trout use its lateral line? Information from this organ might be useful in detecting the position of stationary and moving objects in the vicinity, and lateral lines may respond to vibrating waves at the water's surface (Bleckmann 1993).

Although little seems to be known about how trout might locate stationary objects around them by means of the lateral line, as we might expect, such an ability is well developed in certain blind cave fish. Such fish have been observed to swim swiftly toward and then glide past newly encountered objects. By doing so, they produce a flow field around themselves and are apparently able to detect object-induced distortions to this field by comparing the responses of their hair cells at different locations on their lateral line.

Moving objects of importance to trout consist of predators, prey, and competitors of the same and other species. A swimming fish produces a complicated series of currents and eddies that are probably detectable by another fish several meters and a number of seconds removed. Presumably, a fish could detect and evaluate the producer of such a vortex trail either by swimming through it in still water or as it sweeps past in the stream's flow. Although little is known about such an ability, it could produce much information about the size, direction, and speed of other animals.

Evidence that fish use their lateral line to detect prey comes from several studies of nonsalmonids but provides considerable indirect evidence that the ability exists in trout as well. Even when blinded, pike could detect and attack moving prey fish from as far as 10 cm away but lost this ability if researchers also destroyed their lateral line organs (Wunder 1927).

Cobalt ions are known to block the functioning of the lateral line without affecting a fish's motivation to feed. Sunfish are insensitive to infrared light but can still catch prey fish when only infrared light is available. However, after researchers blocked the lateral lines of sunfish, under infrared they attacked prey only if they bumped into them by accident. This study (Karlsen and Sand 1987) capitalized on the reversibility of cobalt to demonstrate elegantly that after recovery of their lateral line function, the blinded sunfish could again find prey. It would be quite interesting to have the results of similar work with salmonids.

Of particular interest to the student of trout is how fish living in moving water use their lateral line. As I will show later, much work on trout foraging and habitat selection has emphasized how energy output and food intake are affected by a fish's position relative to current speed. Note here that salmonids are exquisitely attuned, via their lateral line organs, to minute variation in water flow and turbulence. While it might seem that vision would be necessary to hold position in a stream, brook trout can hold behind an obstacle to current flow even in complete darkness (Sutterlin and Waddy 1975). Furthermore, the trout lose this night-time ability if the nerve connections to the hind sections of both lateral line organs are cut. The threshold current in which brook trout could no longer maintain position, and were swept downstream, was 47 cm per second (1.03 mph) in the absence of obstacles. In darkness intact fish could remain in currents as strong as 86 cm per second (1.89 mph) by sheltering behind small obstacles, but this ability was severely diminished by loss of lateral line function. Fish in darkness and without lateral lines could not maintain position behind sheltering obstacles and therefore could not hold position in flows greater than 51 cm per second (1.12 mph). It thus appears that the neuromasts of the rearmost portion of the lateral line are important in informing a trout about the speed and direction of currents, allowing it to conserve energy in relatively quiet water even amid a torrent.

Because trout have a delightful propensity to feed at the water surface, the information that they might obtain from surface waves is of interest. Surface waves move through water at its boundary with the air. The first salient property of these waves is that they carry much farther where air and water meet than within the water column itself. Furthermore, attenuation of surface waves is related to their frequency, with high frequencies, such those that a struggling insect might produce, attenuating most rapidly. For example, insects struggling on the surface vibrate their wings at a frequency of 50 to 140 Hz. (It is surely not by coincidence that certain surface-feeding fish other than trout are most sensitive to frequencies of the same range [Bleckmann et al. 1989].) At the point where vibrations of 140 Hz have penetrated 2.9 cm below the surface, the vertical movement induced in water molecules is only

2% of the movement at the surface. Such drastic attenuation of surface waves with depth could explain why trout often hang so close beneath a drifting insect or dry fly when inspecting it.

The evidence is good that some surface-feeding fish can determine the direction and distance to the source of surface waves solely by analyzing the mechanical properties of the waveform. Apparently, such fish detect direction by comparing simultaneous mechanical stimulation at different locations on their lateral lines. Researchers have advanced several ideas about how such fish might determine distance to a prey insect. One interesting possibility is that fish memorize the vibration frequency of a particular species of water-trapped insect. Then, having learned the rate at which that frequency attenuates with distance, the fish can use the strength of the vibration that it perceives to predict how far away the insect is. Using a quite clever technique, Bleckmann (1988) showed that topminnows overshot a target location by a greater distance as the generated frequency of constant amplitude increased. That is, the fish appeared to "know" that at a given perceived amplitude, a higher-frequency source should be closer than a lower-frequency source. Bleckmann's vibratory stimulus was nothing more than a puff of air blown vertically down on the water surface. Thus the fish could tell him where they thought the source of the vibration was in the absence of any confounding object in the water. We have little evidence about how trout use surface waves.

Smell and Taste

The third principal means by which trout monitor the world around them is through the chemical senses of smell and taste. The chemical sensory organs lie on the external surface, making them readily accessible for study. Thus we now have quite a good idea of what classes of chemicals trout perceive and where in the central nervous system they send such information (Hara 1994).

The chemical senses are intimately associated with two prime biological functions, feeding and reproduction. In fish it is often hard to differentiate between olfaction and gustation. A distinction between the two systems says that nerves carry information from terminal sensory structures to the brain. If such information is carried by the first cranial nerve, the receptor must be olfactory. If impulses reach the brain from peripheral receptors via nerves other than the first cranial, such receptors are classified as taste receptors.

In fish the olfactory organs are found on the upper surface of the head near the front of the animal and have no connection with the inside of the mouth. As a fish swims or as it holds position in a current, water flows into and through a channel in each olfactory organ. Lining the inside of the channel, often covering folds or crenelations, is the olfactory epithelium, a double layer containing receptor cells, the actual cells receptive to chemical stimulation, and two types of supporting cells. Each receptor cell is directly exposed to the water and terminates in an axon, a long nerve-cell process, that extends all the way from the olfactory organ to the olfactory bulb of the brain.

Each of the two olfactory organs has 5 to 10 million receptor cells. These cells are unique among vertebrate nerve cells in that they can be regenerated within about a week if cut or killed with chemicals (Moran et al. 1992). Indeed, such cells die and are replaced continually during the normal life of a trout.

Within the olfactory bulb of its brain, synapses transfer information from axons coming from the olfactory organ to a second group of cells called the *mitral cells*. The mitral cells, in turn, relay messages about chemicals in the environment to other centers in the brain. As part of this transfer, an interesting summation of information must occur—while axons from 5 to 10 million receptor cells enter each olfactory bulb, the number of mitral cells is 1,000 times fewer.

Beyond the scope of this book are the biochemical details of how a chemical signal received by a receptor cell is transduced into an electrical signal sent to the brain (Brand and Bruch 1992). However, what is detected is fascinating. From physiological studies monitoring electrical impulse traffic in axons of receptor cells, we know that trout can smell four broad categories of odors: amino acids, sex steroids, bile acids or salts, and prostaglandins.

Amino acids are complex organic compounds that serve as the building blocks of proteins. We can readily imagine that a carnivorous animal like a trout would be well served by an ability to detect odors related to protein. And trout are staggeringly good at such detection, being sensitive to concentrations of odors of about 10^{-8} molar. This means that trout can detect 1 molecule of an amino acid diluted in 10 billion molecules of water. Certain amino acids, such as L-proline, L-alanine (see figure 2.3), and L-leucine, have been shown to operate through the olfactory system to induce or arouse the swimming, turning, and biting behavior of feeding in adult rainbow trout (Valentincic and Caprio 1997). (Of course, it would not be at all sporting to soak a muddler minnow with L-alanine.)

Although reproductive biology is not the main focus of this work, it is worth noting that salmonids can be highly sensitive to the existence of sex steriods. For example, sexually mature male Atlantic salmon can detect testosterone at concentrations of 10^{-14} molar (10^{-14} molar = 1 molecule of testosterone per 10 million billion molecules of water). Brown trout have been shown to be sensitive to only one of more than 100 different sex steroids tested, a compound called etiocholanolone glucuronide (Essington and Sorensen 1996; Sorensen and Caprio 1998).

Bile acids are steroidal compounds whose prime function seems to be the emulsification of ingested fats. Although bile acids are generally reabsorbed within the excretory system, some are also released to the environment, where they can be detected by the olfactory system of other fish. Sorensen and his colleagues have tested brown trout against 42 different bile acids, finding a sensitivity to four (Sorensen and Caprio 1998). Certain salmonids are exquisitely sensitive to bile acids. Sorensen and Caprio demonstrated that rainbow trout can perceive one particular bile acid at concentrations of 10^{-12} to 10^{-11} molar (about one part in a hundred trillion), a concentration 10,000 times less than the species' threshold sensitivity to amino acids.

Prostaglandins are fatty acids that commonly act as hormones within the body. However, brown trout, at least, can detect several different prostaglandins in their external environment that may act as reproductive pheromones (Sorensen and Caprio 1998).

Different types of receptors detect the four classes of chemical stimulants. Interestingly, although the various types of receptor seem to be distributed randomly across the olfactory epithelium, their axons sort themselves out so that they synapse with mitral cells in different regions of the olfactory bulb.

Material concerning migratory behavior will not be a major component of this book, but I will discuss migration at appropriate points.

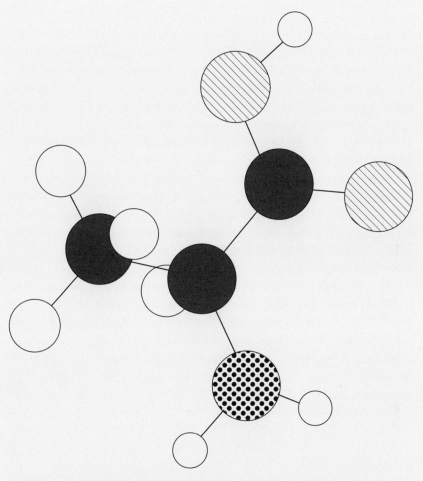

Figure 2.3. Molecular Configuration of the Amino Acid L-alanine. L-alanine is one of several amino acids that have been shown to act through the smell and taste systems to arouse the feeding behavior of trout. The solid circles are carbon atoms; the stippled circle represents nitrogen; cross-hatching shows the two oxygen atoms; and the clear circles represent hydrogen. (After Sorenson and Caprio 1998)

Because olfaction is an important factor in migratory behavior, this is one of those points. The migratory cycle of salmon and sea trout has three phases: the downstream movement to the sea (or large lake), the return of sexually mature adults to the vicinity of the outlet of the natal stream, and the migration up the home stream (Hara 1993). Although the initial movement downstream from the birth site seems largely explainable as the product of a taxis or genetically controlled movement, as I mentioned earlier, researchers think that sun compass orientation may be one mechanism controlling the direction of movements on the high seas, including the return path to the mouth of the natal stream. Olfactory navigation comes into play in the upstream return to the precise birth tributary, where spawning occurs. Later, I will discuss this ability, one of the more amazing phenomena of nature, in conjunction with imprinting.

Taste, the second chemical sensory system, has as its functional unit the taste bud. In fishes such as catfish and other habitual bottom feeders, taste buds are widely distributed over the surface of the body, even occurring on the fins. However, in the salmonids taste buds are confined to an area in and around the mouth, reaching a density of 30 taste buds per mm^2 on the palate. Within a taste bud gustatory cells sensitive to chemicals are intermingled with supporting cells. Because the gustatory cell is an epithelial cell rather than a nerve cell, it does not send its own axon to the central nervous system. Instead, gustatory cells stimulate closely applied nerve cells to send impulses centrally.

Sorenson and Caprio (1998) have studied extensively the gustatory response of taste buds to amino acids. Apparently, char are sensitive to only three amino acids, whereas other salmonids are more catholic in their detection abilities.

Magnetic Sense

Salmonids have recently taken a prominent position in research concerning a magnetic sense. Perception of the earth's magnetic field is now thought quite a plausible navigational aid used by salmon and sea-going trout in their large-scale movements to and from the home stream. Before exploring recent findings on such navigation, it will be worthwhile to discuss briefly the characteristics of the earth's magnetic field that could be of use to a navigating fish.

Any magnetic field consists of a closed loop around a current that is moving through a conductor. In the case of the earth's magnetic field, movement of current occurs within the molten core of the earth (Nair et al. 1989). In the earth's magnetic field lines of induction emerge throughout the southern magnetic hemisphere and enter the earth over the northern magnetic hemisphere. The north and south magnetic poles are simply the points on the earth's surface where the lines of inductive force are vertical. The axis of the magnetic field is offset about 15° from the earth's axis of rotation.

Three attributes of the earth's magnetic field could provide information useful to a navigating fish: inclination, declination, and field intensity. Inclination is the angle that the field force lines make with the horizontal and varies between zero degrees at the equator and 90° at the poles. Declination is the horizontal angle between magnetic north and true geographical north. In the eastern United States, the magnetic field declination is about 15°. That is, north, as indicated by a compass needle, is about 15° west of true north (Richards et al. 1960).

The final factor that may cue trout is the intensity of the magnetic field. Field intensity doubles between the equator and the poles, increasing about 6 gauss per northward kilometer in the eastern United States (Gould 1982). As humans cannot perceive magnetic fields and have no intuitive feeling for what a gauss is, an example or two might be useful. At a distance of 0.1 m (about 4 in.), the intensity of the magnetic field around an operating toaster is about 0.1 gauss. At 100 m (about 325 ft.) the magnetic field around a 500 kV transmission line is about 0.01 gauss (Nair et al. 1989).

A salmon might be able to determine its longitude (east-west location) on the face of the earth if it could detect the declination of the earth's field, and it might be able to determine its latitude (north-south location) if it could detect either magnetic field inclination or intensity. In parallel with researchers studying such other animals as honeybees and birds, fish researchers have been exploring the possibility of a magnetic sense in salmon and trout. Here I review briefly how the salmonid work is progressing.

Early results (Quinn et al. 1981) showed that sockeye salmon fry from a stream emptying along the southern shore of Lake Washington in Washington State had an apparently genetically fixed preference to face north in a test tank, even at night and even when the tank was covered with black plastic to rule out any navigation by star position. The young fish were thought to be orienting by the horizontal component of the earth's field. Although work with other kinds of animals had suggested that magnetite, a mineral sensitive to the earth's magnetic field, could be involved in field detection, magnetized material was found in only 4 of 30 fry tested and in such minute quantity that Quinn's team attributed it to contamination of samples. In summing up these results, Quinn and his colleagues suggested that whatever the sensory system was that detected the earth's field, it probably used some system originally evolved for another sensory function. As I will show, this suggestion has apparently turned out to be correct.

Seven years later a study of adult sockeye salmon, rather than fry, detected magnetically sensitive material in the form of magnetite crystals within the cartilage of the ethmoid bone of the skull (Mann et al. 1988). Magnetite is a ferromagnetic mineral consisting of iron and oxygen atoms, Fe_3O_4. Such crystals were about 48 nm (48 billionths of a meter) in size and were arranged in chains bound by organic material. The finding that the crystals were aligned in chains was important. *Torque* is a term that physicists use to describe the rotational force about an axis. If we imagine that each crystal generates torque as it attempts to align with the magnetic field surrounding a fish, the chain alignment means that the total torque produced will be the sum of the torques of individual crystals—and the longer the chain, the more the aggregate torque.

Not long after, Chew and Brown (1989) added two interesting chapters to the story. They showed that nonanadromous (i.e., nonmigratory) rainbow trout were oriented to the earth's magnetic field but became randomly oriented when shielded from exposure to the earth's field. Thus the magnetic sense is not limited to populations of salmonids that are migratory. Second, large trout from this nonmigratory population seemed to agree more closely on which direction to orient than did small trout. That is, the spread of headings of individual fish around the average heading was narrower in the larger animals (see figure 2.4). It is known that the length of crystal chains grows as a fish grows (Mann et al. 1988), and because the torques of all the crystals in a chain apparently can be summed, it may be that the longer crystal chains in larger trout were somehow sending a clearer signal to the brain about the prevailing characteristics of the earth's field. The rainbow trout tested were from a commercial breeder in Alberta and maintained a heading more or less northeast of true north when tested near the city of Lethbridge in the same Canadian province. Patterns of

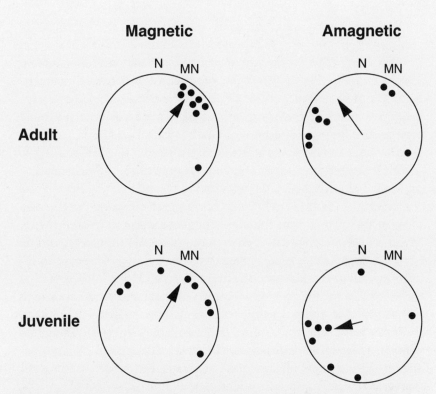

Figure 2.4. Magnetic Orientation in Rainbow Trout. The circle plots display compass orientations of adult and juvenile rainbow trout in the presence of a normal magnetic field and when the magnetic field around the trout is eliminated by a shield of copper wire screening. An environment devoid of all magnetic intensity is termed *amagnetic*. Each dot represents the compass heading of an individual fish. The arrow is the mean heading vector of a group of fish. That is, the direction of the arrow is the average heading direction of a group, and the length of the arrow reflects how closely the fish in each group agreed on a heading direction. For example, an arrow touching the circle means that all fish in the group headed in precisely the same direction. When the fish were exposed to the normal magnetic field, the arrow for the adult trout was longer—adults agreed more closely on a heading direction than did juvenile trout. When the magnetic field was eliminated, the headings of both groups became random, as reflected in the short arrows. (After Chew and Brown 1989)

preferred headings of different genetic stocks of rainbow trout and other salmonids will be worth investigating. Furthermore, potential genetic differences in magnetic field responses are quite worrisome because farmed stocks of salmon do escape and interbreed with locally adapted wild fish.

Recently, Walker and colleagues (1997) used rainbow trout to investigate several loose ends in regard to biomagnetic sensitivity. First, in support of earlier work with the species, juvenile rainbows demonstrated that they could detect the presence of a disturbed magnetic field. The disturbance, termed an *anomaly*, consisted of the experimenters' artificially increasing the local magnetic field intensity around a target bar from 55 microtesla to 125 microtesla (1 tesla = 10,000 gauss). After only about three training sessions, the fish learned to bump the target bar either in the natural or artificial field, depending on which field was associated with a food reward.

Recording impulse traffic in nerves led to the discovery of the next piece of the puzzle. When researchers increased or decreased the intensity of the magnetic field surrounding the head of a trout, certain nerve cells in the ros V nerve (a so-called cranial nerve, not a spinal nerve) sent nerve impulses to the brain. Even with this finding, still remaining was the mystery of which organ first detects the change in magnetic field intensity. The solution turned out to be in the trout's nose.

In the nose of a trout are several lamellae, or folds of tissue, that contain, as expected, cells sensitive to chemical stimuli. Each lamella is actually two layers of olfactory cells separated by a structure called the *lamina propria*. Researchers found that chains of magnetite crystals, similar to those found earlier in sockeye salmon, are situated within the lamina propria of rainbow trout. Furthermore, fine processes of the ros V nerve penetrate the nasal capsule and come to lie close to the cells that bear magnetite crystals (Walker et al. 1997).

So the question of how trout detect geomagnetic fields seems at least partially answered. They monitor field intensity by using magnetite crystals embedded within support tissue in the nasal capsule. However, we do not yet have a good understanding of exactly how the ros V nerve endings are stimulated by torque generated in the magnetite crystal chain. Other questions of a more ecological nature remain. Is magnetic field detection of any use to stream-dwelling trout, animals that never undertake long-distance migratory movements? More to the point, can all trout populations detect magnetic fields? Do they all have magnetite crystal chains? Is there any pattern in preferred orientation to magnetic fields among disparate populations and species? For example, in nonmigratory species such as the Gila trout, is it possible that magnetite chains have become vestigial over time, like our appendix?

Temperature

Water temperature is critically important for the growth and well-being of salmonids. The extent to which trout and salmon can flourish in various water temperatures is partially determined by whether they have been previously acclimated to such temperatures. Apparently, Atlantic salmon can survive and feed in water warmer than any other salmonid can stand (see figure 2.5), but even this species cannot live for extended periods in water much warmer than 27°C or feed in water warmer than 23°C (Elliot 1991).

While it seems reasonable to think that trout species of the hot, dry American Southwest might have evolved a tolerance for especially warm water, apparently this has not happened. In one experiment temperature-acclimated trout were subjected to increasingly warm water until they were no longer able to remain upright; the researchers took the trout's loss of equilibrium to mean that they had reached the upper critical temperature (Lee and Rinne 1980). In this test the Gila trout of the Southwest had an upper limit of 27°C, no better than either brown or rainbow trout, and only 1° warmer than what brook trout could withstand. However, other populations may be more heat resistant. Individuals of an arid-lands variety of rainbow trout known as redband trout maintained excellent health in a Nevada stream at 28.3°C (Behnke 1991).

Two pieces of information about trout and temperature may relate to cognition. Roberts (1973) found that fish die at water temperatures lower than those sufficient to kill individual cells. Apparently, then, sensitive processes in the nervous system, such as the equilibrium response and perhaps cognition and thinking, are the weak link in temperature accommodation. Thus, aside from matters of growth rate, trout may have good reasons to avoid water that is overly warm.

Counteracting any preference for cool water might be the tendency, under certain circumstances, for trout to make themselves develop a kind of fever. Humans react subconsciously to infection by raising their body temperature by means of the autonomic nervous system. This

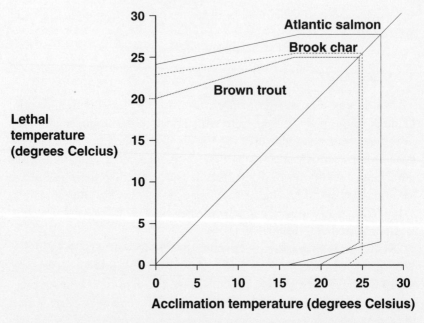

Figure 2.5. Thermal Tolerance of Brook Char, Brown Trout, and Atlantic Salmon. The polygon for each species indicates the range of temperatures across which survival was possible. Within each species fish acclimated to higher temperatures could withstand warmer water. While even warm water–acclimated char and trout became moribund at about 25°C, the salmon could exist in water several degrees warmer still. (After Elliot 1991)

response is thought to be adaptive because the mortality of disease agents increases at elevated body temperature. Covert and Reynolds (1977) determined that goldfish react behaviorally, apparently to accomplish the same goal. Uninfected goldfish preferred to live in water of 27.9° C. However, if infected by injection of living bacteria, the fish shifted their preference to water of 32.7°C. Furthermore, all infected fish allowed to remain at the higher temperature survived, but infected fish suffered considerable mortality if forced to remain in the cooler temperature preferred by uninfected fish. These results strongly suggest that the fish moved to warmer water as an adaptive response to bacterial infection.

Now imagine that trout can operate similarly. How far into potentially lethal temperatures will an infected trout venture? How does it make this decision? This is an example of behavioral trade-offs that occupy a central place in cognitive ecology, the science of why animals think as they do. I must more thoroughly discuss the information that a thinking trout could have at its disposal before we can consider the actual thinking process. In leaving this matter of fever induction, let me suggest that in this area we should be able to observe and experiment in nature with trout that have access to the vicinity of thermal hot springs.

Considering how influential water temperature is in determining growth and survival, it is not surprising that trout are good at detecting temperature changes. Learning psychologists use classical conditioning to investigate various aspects of animal behavior; this is a topic to which I will return in more detail when we consider how trout think. When rainbow trout were trained with a classical conditioning technique (Bardach and Bjorklund 1957), the fish showed that they could detect an increase or decrease in water temperature of as little as 1°C.

Water-Chemistry Perception

Acidity

Acidity refers to the concentration of hydrogen ions (H^+) in water. The index of acidity, pH, takes a value between 0 and 14 and is calculated as the negative logarithm of hydrogen ion concentration. The more acidic the water, the lower the pH.

As a result of the burning of fossil fuels, many lakes and streams not associated with alkaline rock and soil now receive rain and snowmelt that is highly acidic. The extent to which trout can inhabit such acid waters is a large concern in conservation biology. One study focused on the effects of pulsed acidity such as might be experienced by lakes and streams during intermittent thaws (Cleveland et al. 1991). Even when exposed to brief pulses of acidic water only once every 5 days, young brook trout showed considerable reductions in feeding rate, swimming activity, and growth rate.

From the burgeoning literature concerning responses of salmonids to acidification, I include just one other study here, partially as a cautionary tale (Rask et al. 1992). Whitefish were stocked into six Finnish lakes of differing acidity and, not surprisingly, failed to survive in the three most acidic. However, of the three less acidic lakes in which the stocked fish did survive, their growth rate was highest in the most acidic environment. Rask and colleagues invoked an interaction between acidity and interspecific competition to explain this apparent paradox. Perch, which are known to compete for food with whitefish in Finland, were absent from the lake with fastest-growing whitefish but present in the other two.

How trout actually detect the acidity of their environment has not been well studied. Most likely, the olfactory system is directly sensitive to hydrogen ion concentration.

Salinity

Salmon and trout are highly sensitive to salinity. Because all salmonids breed only in freshwater, we have good reason to believe that they have evolved from a freshwater-dwelling ancestor. Nevertheless, salmonids seem to have taken advantage of evolutionary opportunities to include a portion of their life cycle in the oceans, apparently because food supplies and resulting growth rates are so much higher there than in lakes and streams.

The concentration of salts maintained internally by a typical fish is higher than that of freshwater and lower than that of saltwater. Because the same individual salmonid often must deal with both environments during its lifetime, we need to make a brief expedition into the physiology of salt regulation (Evans 1998). Seawater is hyperosmotic compared to fish. This means that positively and negatively charged ions such as sodium and chlorine tend to move down concentration gradients from the environment into the fish, and water tends to move from the fish into the environment. A fish is constantly at risk of drying out while swimming around in seawater. To compensate for the lost water, ocean fish drink copiously, absorb large amounts of seawater across the lining of the intestine, and secrete only small amounts of urine that are relatively high in salt concentrations. However, most salts continuously invading oceanic fish are secreted back to the environment through specialized cells in the gills called *chloride cells*. Using a complicated chemical transportation mechanism that requires energy to operate, chloride cells secrete chloride ions back to the ocean. The sodium ions that we think of as the essence of seawater actually move back to the outside of the fish along passages between the chloride cells. The positively charged sodium ions are eliminated without energy cost to the fish; they just move toward the higher concentrations of negatively charged chloride ions being maintained near the gill surface by the chloride cells.

Salmon and trout in freshwater have the opposite problem. Because their internal environment is more salty than the outside, they tend to be invaded by water. One study showed that incoming water amounted to about 50% of a fish's total body water per hour (Evans 1998). As we might expect, fish in freshwater drink little and excrete large volumes of water from their kidneys. Because salts in freshwater fish tend to be lost to the environment, the kidney reabsorbs most sodium and chloride ions. Although there is some disagreement about the details (Evans 1998), it seems clear that in freshwater fish, cells in the gills actually move positive and negative ions from the water into the fish against a concentration gradient.

In salmon and trout moving between salty and fresh water, some of these physiological processes are reversed, and the reversal seems to be under genetic control. When they grow from the freshwater parr stage to the smolt stage and head downstream to the ocean, young salmon and sea-going trout must change physiologically from hoarding salts and discarding water to the opposite strategy. In one study young Arctic char conditioned to freshwater were exposed for 48 hours to salinity of 25 ppt (Schmitz 1992). Such a concentration might be found in the outer reaches of an estuary, as the salinity of the open ocean is about 35 ppt. During late winter and early spring, when young fish in nature would be moving from freshwater into the ocean to feed for the summer, the char in the experiment secreted sufficient sodium to keep the plasma concentration of sodium about the same as in freshwater-dwelling char. However, during August and September, when wild fish would be moving from estuaries upstream to overwinter in freshwater, blood plasma concentrations of sodium rose dramatically in the captive fish exposed to saline water. Clearly, then, the physiological response to saltwater varied through the year.

Schmitz (1992) took the char for the experiment from a landlocked freshwater population that had had no contact with the sea for at least 6,000 years. The springtime response to high salt concentrations was thus a sort of physiological equivalent to our appendix, a historical remnant with no remaining adaptive value.

We know little about how salmonids actually detect salt concentrations. Some have suggested that the chloride cells themselves detect salinity, although we have no evidence of any sort of nervous connection between chloride cells and the brain. Clearly, though, salmonids can react behaviorally to changes in salinity. In following radio-tagged fish, Terry Haines (personal communication) recently found that during the downstream run, wild Atlantic salmon smolts hesitated upon encountering saltwater, often turning back or remaining in place for some time before continuing on out into the ocean.

Several hormones influence how trout adjust their body's concentration of salts. The uropophysis, a gland located at the tail end of the spinal chord, secretes at least two hormones that promote secretion by chloride cells. Thyroxine, a hormone produced by the thyroid gland, is especially important in smolting, the transition from fresh to saltwater. Among other things, thyroxine promotes the deposition of guanine in the scales, resulting in the change to the shimmering silver color characteristic of salmonids in saltwater. Hormones from the thyroid also influence the osmoregulatory ability of the gills and kidneys. Hormones secreted by such glands as the corpuscles of Stannius, chromaffin tissue, and interrenals also control internal levels of one or more positive and negative ions.

Oxygen

In trout, as in other fishes not able to breathe air directly, exchange of oxygen and carbon dioxide takes place across the body surface. In adults virtually all such exchange occurs across the gills, but in embryos and larvae the major site of such exchange is the overall body surface. Details about how the gills and circulatory system function are not germane here because we are focusing on the information that a trout can acquire about its environment.

The oxygen-holding capacity of water is about twenty-five times lower than that of air, making oxygen much more difficult to obtain in the aqueous medium (Clarke 1954). By contrast, water has a high capacity for holding carbon dioxide, so that fish can easily rid themselves of this waste product of metabolism. The upshot is that fish have evolved to monitor and respond to levels of oxygen rather than to levels of carbon dioxide, as is the case for terrestrial organisms breathing air (Gilmour 1998). The receptors for monitoring oxygen supply are most probably in the brain (Bamford 1974) and most likely respond to changes in the concentration or rate of delivery of oxygen in the bloodstream.

Trout and other fish respond to a reduction in oxygen supply (called *hypoxia*) by increasing the volume of water moved across the gills with each coordinated movement of mouth and operculum. That is, they process more water per gulp but do not much increase the rate of gulping (Shezifi et al. 1997).

Temperature and, to a lesser extent, salinity are the primary mechanisms that control the amount of gas that water can hold. That is why carbonated beverages in open containers remain fizzier if kept chilled. In fact, water at 30°C holds only about half as much oxygen as water at 0°C. Thus trout are exposed to double jeopardy. While the rate that oxygen is consumed by metabolism increases with temperature, the oxygen available decreases. Some detrimental effects of high temperature may actually result from hypoxia.

Salinity also influences the oxygen-holding capacity of water. At 15°C a liter of freshwater can hold 7.2 cc of oxygen, but at the same temperature a liter of seawater can hold only 5.8 cc of oxygen, a 19% decrease (Clarke 1954). So we can envision a complicated system in which, for example, the most oxygen is to be found in the coolest, freshest water. Love (1970) even found that as young salmon smolts move downstream into brackish and then saltwater, they change their hemoglobin to a variety with a higher affinity for oxygen.

Chapter 3

Internal Factors

Trout thinking is influenced not only by external factors but by the fish's internal environment. Whereas external factors may vary for short periods, for example at the speed of sound or light, the internal factors generally change at a much slower pace, a period of minutes or even months. Because of this difference internal factors have been termed *slow-process factors* (Heiligenberg 1974). Although they operate in a much different time frame, internal factors are important forces that influence the thinking and behavior of trout. One obvious example is that how hungry a fish is determines its decisions about what, when, and where to eat. I begin this chapter by considering biological rhythms or cycles, then turn to consideration of the metabolic cost of living and related issues concerning hunger state.

Biological Rhythms

Biological rhythms are regular physiological and/or behavioral oscillations in an animal (Gerkema 1992). In some cases the regularity of the timing, or periodicity, of such oscillations does not depend on any external cue from the environment. Such rhythms are termed *endogenous rhythms*, which means that they are completely internal. Animals of the same species living in the same place usually have endogenous rhythms that vary around some average oscillation. That is why such rhythms are called *circa-rhythms*. Noncirca-rhythms are not endogenous and instead simply follow some regularly recurring environmental cue such as light intensity or environmental temperature. A central question concerning rhythms has been whether the many biological rhythms now known are endogenous in the timing of their oscillations or whether such timing is simply the result of an animal's adaptation to the regular oscillation of some environmental cue, such as light intensity.

People often assume that endogenous rhythms are the result of natural selection because they allow an animal to prepare for regular environmental change by adjusting such attributes as enzymatic activity, quantity of energy reserves, and sensitivity of photoreceptors (Gerkema 1992). Trout and salmon show evidence of endogenous rhythms that are both yearly (circannual) or daily (circadian). Many cycles with other periodicities have been identified elsewhere in the animal kingdom (Huntingford 1984).

In migratory salmon and trout, smolting, or smoltification, is the sequence of physiological and behavioral changes that causes a young stream-dwelling fish, a parr, to become a smolt, an animal that will head downstream and enter a large lake or ocean. At adulthood such a fish will then return to its natal stream to breed. Certain aspects of smolting, often mediated by thyroxine, appear to depend on an endogenous circannual process (Eriksson et al. 1982; Eriksson 1984). For example, in Atlantic salmon parr too young to smolt, the level of swimming activity per day closely followed the annual variation in day length and water temperature (figure 3.1). However, during June, when somewhat larger parr turn into smolts and run to the sea, captive smoltsize parr showed a sudden and 100% increase in swimming behavior. Furthermore, in captive animals, after the brief June pulse, swimming behavior in smoltsize parr dropped back to the pre-pulse level. The explanation given by Eriksson and Lundqvist (1982) was that such a heightened level of swimming behavior is controlled endogenously and is adaptive in getting smolt downstream to the sea as rapidly as possible. Predation risk is likely to be lower in the ocean than in unfamiliar reaches of streams. However, an animal that for some reason does not reach the sea can then revert to stream-dwelling behavior, perhaps delaying smolting until the following year. Young salmon housed for 14 months under constant regimes of light and temperature provided convincing evidence for a circannual rhythm of smolting. Under such conditions fish began the anatomical and physiological changes associated with smolting at an interval of 10 months, instead of the 12-month interval shown by fish entrained to photoperiod in nature (Eriksson and Lundqvist 1982).

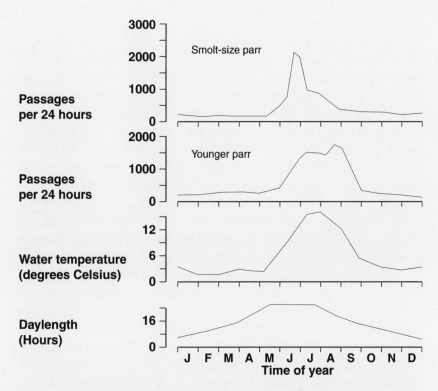

Figure 3.1. Relationship of Swimming Intensity, Water Temperature, and Day Length for Captive Young Atlantic Salmon. As the top graph shows, smolt-size parr displayed a sudden increase in swimming frequency during June, when such fish in the wild would be heading downstream to the sea. Smaller parr too young to go to sea did not display this behavior, so the swimming was interpreted as being endogenously controlled (that is, controlled by internal factors). For the younger fish, swimming intensity seemed to be influenced more by locally occurring water temperature and number of hours of daylight. (After Eriksson et al. 1982)

Another characteristic of young salmon that appears to follow a circannual pattern is the response to salt concentrations (Baggerman 1960; Eriksson 1984). Near the time of downstream migration, smolt-parr of several species of Pacific salmon showed a preference for salty over freshwater. In coho and sockeye the preference was reversible. If held in captivity beyond the normal smolting period in the spring, young fish reverted to a preference for freshwater through the following summer, fall, and winter, only to again prefer saltwater the following spring (Baggerman 1960).

The salt concentration of the water interacts with the circannual rhythm of smolts. In freshwater captive Atlantic salmon smolts swam "downstream" and remained high in the water column only during May and June. After that period they reverted to the stream-dwelling behavior of remaining near the bottom and facing into the current. By contrast, smolts from the same hatchery batch that were housed in brackish water (25 parts of salt per 1,000) continued swimming down-stream and remained high in the water column throughout the course of a year (Eriksson 1984). The behavior of the brackish-water group accords well with what is known of smolts after they reach estuaries. Salty water is not necessary for smoltlike behavior, as attested to by all the populations of salmonids that undergo smolting movements to lakes rather than oceans. Even so, the genetic basis for a circannual rhythm in response to saline water is prominent. Arctic char in a pop-ulation that for about 6,000 years has been cut off from any access to the sea still show a seasonal response to seawater (Schmitz 1992).

Smolting occurs in salmon of different ages even within the same natal stream. Some male Atlantic salmon born in a stream never go to sea at all, instead remaining in the home stream and becoming sexually mature at a young age and small size. Circannual rhythms of smolting clearly will influence how a salmon or trout processes information about food resources and other habitat characteristics. A smolt-parr on its way to the ocean is no longer paying much attention, if any, to distribution patterns of drifting mayflies or comparing flow velocities across potential holding stations.

The life of a trout includes many other annual patterns—of food selection, activity, habitat selection, and so on. However, most such patterns appear to be the result of noncirca-rhythms. That is, they are not endogenous but are entrained to the periodicity of external cues. For example, in northern Sweden salmon parr were most active around noon in January and around midnight in June. However, this large dif-ference was explainable by entrainment. The parr were crepuscular in activity, meaning that they were most active at dawn and dusk. It so happens that in the far north of Sweden only one short period of low light intensity occurs each day in both January and June. In January that light period is around solar noon and in June around solar mid-night. By contrast, in March, when Sweden has a true dawn and true dusk, the parr showed two corresponding peaks of activity (Eriksson and Lundqvist 1982).

Although many physiological and behavioral attributes of trout follow a daily cycle, only a few have been shown unequivocally to be circadian. In many fish species one such circadian function is the secretion of melatonin by the pineal organ. The pineal gland is found just under the upper surface of the skull and has connections with the diencephalon of the brain. Although it normally synthesizes melatonin during the dark phase of the daily cycle, the pineal organ continues a circadian pattern of secretion even in noncycling light intensities (Ligo et al. 1991). The melatonin synchronizes physiological systems with the prevailing day-night cycle.

Apparently, of the many fish species investigated to date, only the pineal gland of rainbow trout (and presumably other salmonids so far untested) does not show endogenous activity; it is entrained to the existing environmental light-dark cycle (Gern et al. 1992). Instead, in trout several physiological properties of the retina apparently cycle in circadian fashion (Zaunreiter et al. 1998), indicating that the eye may have a biological clock that is on about a 24-hour cycle. Movements of both cones and rod-shielding pigments showed circadian periodicities even when the trout were kept in constant darkness. Also, within the retina, concentrations of melatonin and dopamine, two chemical compounds generally associated with circadian characteristics of the retina, cycled over a 24-hour period, even in constant darkness.

The dawn and dusk pattern of feeding in trout is well known to anglers. Two studies have found an endogenous element to the pattern (Cuenca and Delahiguera 1994). Rainbow trout held under constant light conditions maintained either a 25.3-hour (Cuenca and Delahiguera 1994) or a 26.2-hour (Sánchez-Vázquez and Tabata 1998) circadian pattern of food consumption.

When trout are in concealment, rather than out and about, what are they doing? Are they sleeping? Meddis (1975) has suggested that sleeping in a refuge during periods of low food availability or high predation risk is adaptive because it allows an animal both to conserve energy and to reduce predation risk.

It is not so easy to tell when a fish is asleep (Reebs 1992). Electrocardiograms taken from the cortex are used to detect brain waves characteristic of sleep in birds and mammals. But fish have no cortex and live in an aqueous environment where it is hard to obtain ECGs. What about prolonged closure of the eyes? No good: fish lack eyelids. Students of fish sleep have developed several useful criteria. If a fish remains unmoving in some sort of shelter for a long period and is hard to arouse during that period, it is considered to be asleep.

No relevant experimental work exists on sleep in salmonids. From work with other species it appears that sleep cycles could be endogenous. For example, lake chub maintained a daily cycle of periodic activity and inactivity in constant darkness for 1,520 days, as did immature burbot for 40 days.

Regardless of whether they are endogenously controlled or entrained to an external time giver, trout have been shown to have several other daily cycles. Juvenile rainbow trout wintering in southeastern Idaho spent the daylight hours concealed in crevices in the stream bottom (Contor and Griffith 1995). They emerged from these refuges 30 to 80 minutes after sunset, at a time when the stars first became visible. The reduction in numbers of fish emerging on moonlit nights suggested that these activities were not circadian. The number of drifting invertebrates is higher at night than during the day but is depressed by moonlight (Anderson 1966). Therefore, the behavior of these young trout may be explained by higher risk of predation during the day and on moonlit nights, by lower food supplies under those conditions, or both.

Apparently, it is not only very young trout that hide in streambed gravel during the day. Butler (1991:81) has described large brown trout in a Sierra Nevada stream as bursting from the gravel during the last light of day and "literally swim[ming] into the gravel bottom, head first, and so bury[ing] themselves" at first light in the morning.

Gries and colleagues (1997) have reported the results of a survey by snorkel in several Vermont tributaries of the Connecticut River where operations are underway to restore an Atlantic salmon fishery. During the late summer surveys young-of-year and post–young-of-year salmon, as well as brook trout, had different daily activity periods, with the younger fish more likely to be active during the day (see figure 3.2). In fact, post–young-of-year individuals were active almost exclusively at night. Gries and colleagues (1997) suggested that higher risk of predation during daylight explains the difference between age classes in degree of nocturnality. This explanation is not entirely satis-

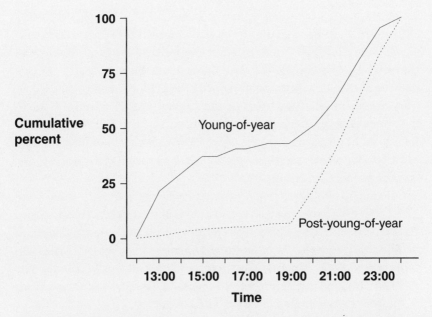

Figure 3.2. Late-Day Stream Swimming by Atlantic Salmon. The graphs show the cumulative percent occurrence of young-of-year and post–young-of-year Atlantic salmon in several Vermont streams during the afternoon and evening. For each hourly period the steeper the slope of a line, the more fish were sighted by snorkelers. In general, young-of-year fish became active earlier in the day, whereas their older brethren did not venture from shelter until after dark. (After Gries et al. 1997)

factory, as one would think that little fish are more susceptible to predators than larger ones, not the reverse.

Energy and Metabolism

We have reason to think that natural selection should favor trout that grow as fast as possible. Growth, of course, competes with the metabolic cost of existence for incoming energy and nutrients. As part of the consideration of internal factors influencing trout thinking and behavior, I will now discuss in some detail the metabolism, or energetics, of trout. While researchers recognize that specific nutrients such as vitamins and minerals can limit growth and reproduction, they often assume, as I do here, that a diet adequate in energy content will also be adequate in specific nutrients.

What happens to the food energy ingested by a trout? Each joule

(J) of energy (0.24 calories) taken in can end up in one of four places (Elliot 1994). First, because the processing of food is not 100% efficient, some energy passes undigested through the trout and emerges in the feces. Second, energy is lost in the form of the excretory products, ammonia and urea (Lauf and Wood 1996). Third, energy is used to maintain metabolic functions of the various organ systems. Fourth, and finally, energy can augment the total energy value of the body materials, including somatic mass, eggs, sperm, and semen. Because this last category relates quite directly to lifetime reproductive success, it is close to natural selection's bottom line.

The energy required for metabolic processes falls into three categories. Some of this energy, used in so-called standard metabolism, supports life functions at the level required by a quiet, resting fish that is not digesting food. A second component of the energy, termed *activity metabolism,* supports swimming and other forms of activity. The third and final portion of metabolic energy, called *feeding metabolism,* is required by the processes of food digestion.

Let us assume that natural selection favors channeling as much ingested food as possible into body growth, eggs, or sperm. How might trout biology conform to such selection? The proportion of ingested energy that is lost in feces and urine is not likely to be much under the control of an individual trout, although the former does vary to some extent with the amount of food eaten. Likewise, the metabolic cost of digestion is pretty well fixed for any level of food ingestion. So the portions of its energy budget that a trout might be able to control to a considerable extent are its standard metabolic rate and its metabolic cost of activity.

In physiology the so-called Q_{10} rule (Davson 1964) states that metabolic processes double in rate with every rise in temperature of 10°C. This means, for example, that the standard metabolism of a cold-blooded animal such as a trout uses twice as much energy at 15°C as at 5°C and four times as much energy at 25°C as at 5°C. Thus a trout could adjust its metabolic expenditure a great deal by choosing among water temperatures in which to live.

Lest you conclude that saving energy by staying at low temperatures is always best, remember that the Q_{10} rule applies to all metabolic processes, including digestion. Suppose a trout living in very cold water has access to unlimited food. Under such conditions its rate of growth will be limited by the rate at which it can digest that food. For example, a captive 50-g brown trout fed all it wanted was found to add 1,000 calories' worth of growth per day at 12.8°C but less than 100 calories' worth of growth at 3.8°C (Elliot 1976). The difference occurred because at the lower temperature, the rate at which food could be digested limited growth. Having access to unlimited amounts of food does no good if a fish cannot digest that food rapidly.

This matter of digestion rates and food quantities brings us to consider the issue of trade-offs, an issue that will dominate this book's approach to trout thinking. I have related how when food is readily accessible, temperature-dependent digestion rates limit trout growth. However, consider a case where food is completely unavailable. In such a case the trout will starve, but because its metabolism is a function of temperature, it will starve most slowly at the lowest temperature it can find. So within physiological tolerances, if you are a trout, you live in the warmest temperatures you can find if food is unlimited and in the coldest temperatures you can find if food is absent. Now, the important point is that food is almost never unlimited and seldom completely absent. I assume that there is some optimal relationship between food supply and temperature at which a trout will grow the fastest. I also assume that natural selection has fashioned trout that attempt to live where this optimal relationship occurs (Hughes 1992a, 1992b, 1998).

In addition to water temperature, muscular exertion during swimming influences a trout's metabolic rate. An important feature of the trout-feeding experiment by Elliott (1976) is that captive animals were fed all they wanted in aquaria with essentially no current so that activity metabolism was held at a minimum. Several other studies have examined metabolic responses to systematically varied current speed when trout were forced to maintain station. Although swimming against a current obviously is more energetically expensive than not, determining how the amount of the expense varies with current speed is interesting. We can imagine that if significant variation exists, trout may have been selected to take current speed into account when deciding where to rest or forage for food.

Several studies have addressed the effect of current speed on metabolic rates of salmonids (Brett and Glass 1973; Beamish 1980; Smith and Li 1983). We will examine the research by Lauf and Wood (1996) in some detail. Juvenile rainbow trout weighing 8 to 10 g were allowed to swim against a current in a closed circular tank in which the water temperature was held constant at 15°C. For most of a 58-hour period each fish swam in freshly oxygenated water. Periodically, the supply of freshly oxygenated water was shut off, after which the fish continued to swim while depleting the oxygen in the closed system. After half an hour of such conditions freshly oxygenated water was again admitted to the system. By comparing oxygen concentrations in the water at the start and end of each closed-system period, the researchers were able to calculate the amount of oxygen consumed. Because the relationship between oxygen consumption and energy consumption is known, Lauf and Wood could convert the results to joules. (One joule is the amount of heat required to raise the temperature of 0.24 cc of water 1°C.) During the 58-hour period the energetic cost of swimming against any particular current speed gradually decreased, but the investigators noted that this result could have been the result of the animals' gradually becoming accustomed to the test chamber. In any case, assuming that the cost-of-swimming value at the end of 58 hours would most closely approximate the cost to a wild trout living permanently in a stream, I have concentrated on the 58-hour values.

Each fish had been starved for 48 hours before its trial began, so the metabolism of feeding (i.e., digestion) during a trial was considered negligible. In water with no current the fish expended energy at the rate of 13.3 J per gram of body weight per hour. This cost might be considered the standard metabolism (figure 3.3).

The researchers standardized current speed in terms of body lengths per unit of time, a common practice in such research. Trout forced to swim continuously against a current of 2.1 body lengths per second spent 17.0 J per gram of body mass per hour. The increase of 3.7 J per gram per hour represented a 28% increment in metabolic cost over activity in calm water. Finally, when the current was raised to 3.1 body lengths per second, metabolism increased to 28.5 J per gram per hour, an increase of 117% over swimming in calm water.

We have some evidence that metabolic rate can be affected by factors other than water temperature and current speed. For example, Facey and Grossman (1990) held rainbow trout under similar condi-

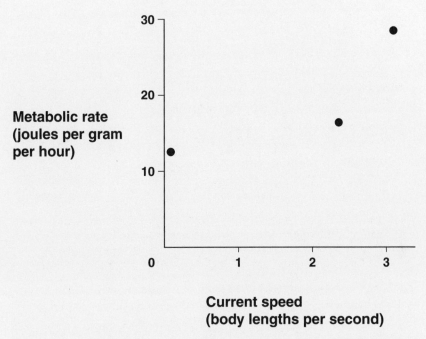

Figure 3.3. Metabolic Rates of Juvenile Rainbow Trout Holding in Varying Currents. Researchers standardized the current speed to the body length of the test fish. The units on the y-axis are joules of energy consumed per gram of body tissue per hour of swimming (1 J = 0.24 calories). When trout held position in a current that was passing them at a rate of 3 body lengths per second, they metabolized energy reserves at more than twice the rate as in still water. (After Lauf and Wood 1996)

tions of current speed and temperature and found that they had somewhat higher metabolic rates in the autumn than in the spring, a difference for which the researchers offered no explanation.

These studies point to the great metabolic savings to be had from remaining out of the current. Yet trout in streams seem, of course, to do very much the opposite. For example, one study in the Río Negro in Spain found that throughout the year brown trout held station in currents faster than the average for the stream (Rincón and Lobón-Cerviá 1993) (see figure 3.4).

Ah, you say, current speed is not the only factor. What about the rate at which the food supply reaches trout at various current speeds? Good point. Activity metabolism encompasses the cost of remaining at

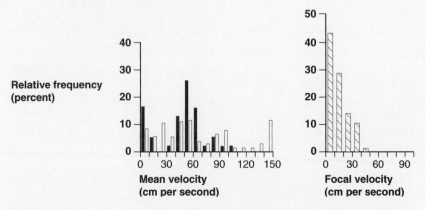

Figure 3.4. Brown Trout Holding Position and Prevailing Current Speeds. The solid bars of the graph at left show that current speeds at many sampling locations in a Spanish river were close to zero, many were in the range of 50 to 70 cm per second, and few were faster than 100 cm per second. By contrast, the open bars in the graph at left appear to show that trout seemed to much prefer holding in the few locations with fast current and that they therefore spent more energy for metabolizing than they could have. However, although current speeds were sampled about midway between the top and the bottom of the stream, researchers found that the trout tended to stay closer to the bottom as the midstream current increased. The graph at right illustrates the effect of staying close to the bottom; it shows current speed at the location of a position-holding trout's snout. Almost 75% of the fish were holding in currents slower than 20 cm per second. Trout holding near the bottom could remain in slow-moving water even as they watched for food drifting by in the rapid water overhead. (After Rincón and Lobón-Cerviá 1993)

a certain location in a stream, and the energy content of ingested food is a benefit of doing so. Once again, we expect natural selection to favor the optimal balance between costs and benefits, a matter to which we will return in conjunction with trout cognition.

Hunger State

Hunger state is definitely an internal factor, but it is somewhat peculiar in the sense that it can act both as a stimulus that influences behavior and as a consequence of previous behavior. Somewhat arbitrarily, I have included the topic here among internal factors influencing the decision processes of trout, although I recognize that hunger state can also be influenced by previous decisions.

Two questions bear on how hunger state might affect trout cognition. First, how much is a fish motivated to eat? Second, if it is motivated to eat, how does it know whether it is getting enough to eat? Earlier on I assumed that natural selection favors rapid growth because of growth's connection to fitness. While this assumption probably holds generally, natural selection appears to have relaxed its emphasis on growth in several aspects of salmonid life history. Cases where trout stop growing or even lose weight seem to be related to some fitness cost to continued foraging for food.

Elliot (1994) raised brown trout from eggs and followed their growth rates in captivity for two years. Under conditions of excess food and in water temperatures known to be adequate for growth to occur, the young animals continued to eat and grow throughout the period, except for their first winter of life. From October through February of that first year the young fish simply stopped growing, remaining at 3 to 4 g for the duration. Because food was in excess, the only conclusion possible, albeit on the basis of indirect evidence, was that during their first winter—but not during the second winter—the young parr essentially stopped eating, perhaps ingesting only enough food to maintain their weight. From an evolutionary perspective the conclusion must be that in the system that Elliot studied, at least, first-year trout that do not attempt to eat have higher lifetime reproductive success than first-year trout that do attempt to eat. Seasonal anorexia has also been demonstrated for the northern pike (Johnson 1966).

Recent studies of Atlantic salmon in Scotland have found direct evidence for voluntary cessation of feeding (Kadri et al. 1995; Kadri et al. 1997). Young salmon migrate to the ocean where they remain until sexually mature. We now know that such mature fish do not feed while moving back to their natal stream to spawn and, furthermore, that they cease feeding altogether even before leaving the ocean. In captivity female salmon with food available in excess stopped eating during the summer, which was sooner than free-ranging fish of the same age would have begun migrating upstream. Thereafter, the captive females began to lose body weight at a rate of 0.1% per day. Among the captives the anorexia of different individuals set in over 2 months, suggesting that the fish were responding to some endogenous state and not to any environmental cue such as water temperature or day length. If the fish stop feeding after reaching some genetically determined target of growth, what might that target be? A rather complex statistical analysis suggested that the captive salmon stopped feeding when they had reached a certain level of lean body mass. Less firmly related to loss of appetite were the amount of body fat or the size of the gonads.

Why do very young trout and mature salmon stop eating? I discuss this point here because such behavior seems related to some physiological set point rather than to a cognitive process. It appears helpful to adopt a cost-benefit analysis in considering these questions. At both life stages the fish are about to enter an environment of relatively little food, the young trout in winter and the mature fish-eating salmon in a stream environment with, presumably, a lower supply of prey fish than the ocean. Apparently, natural selection has favored young salmonids that give up entirely exposing themselves to the predation that they would risk while foraging in the winter; instead, they remain hidden for months in crevices and under stones (Metcalfe and Thorpe 1992). Similarly, once they have reached some threshold level of body size, mature salmon have apparently been selected to forgo foraging entirely so as not to expend energy better committed to the metabolic demands of migration and spawning.

We imagine natural selection to champion rapid growth, except during relatively brief periods. So mental processes such as learning and memory should lead to behavior that fosters growth. In order to exercise their minds in the service of growing fast, trout must possess some relatively precise way of determining how fast they are growing at any given time. While it is difficult to imagine that trout are able somehow to compare fine-scale measurements of their own length or body mass over time, we do have reason to think that they could continually monitor their own hunger state or appetite. Presumably, if a fish behaves in a way that minimizes its state of hunger, it is also behaving to maximize its growth rate.

How might a trout tell how hungry it is? Little evidence from work with fishes bears directly on this question despite continual calls for research (Peter 1979; Holmgren et al. 1983). Reviewers of fish hunger and appetite spend most of their time discussing findings with mammals, and one comes away from reviewing the mammal literature with the impression that physiological responses associated with hunger are quite complex. However, the general conclusion is that mammals are monitoring two factors. The first is the extent of physical distention of the digestive system, indicated by stretch receptors in the gut lining.

Such information would provide a trout with an indirect measure of the rate at which it is ingesting food. The second measure concerns the level of certain chemical constituents of the blood plasma. Blood glucose is monitored by receptors in the hypothalamus and also perhaps by receptors in the hepatic portal system, the part of the circulatory system that links the small intestine and liver. The pancreas detects glucose levels in the blood and responds by secreting one of two hormones, glucagon or insulin. Glucagon raises blood levels of glucose by stimulating conversion of stored glycogen to glucose. Conversely, insulin lowers blood glucose levels by causing glucose to enter the cells of the body (Bone et al. 1995).

Certain amino acids resemble glucose in stimulating activity in the hypothalamus. In a way not possible for an animal to detect by monitoring gut distention alone, information on blood glucose and amino acid levels could integrate the rate at which these nutrients are being ingested and assimilated in the gut with the rate they are being used in metabolism and growth. Both sorts of information, then, are thought to influence the initiation and prolongation of feeding behavior in mammals.

In fish the same general trends seem to hold. Furthermore, Grove and colleagues (1978) have found that the richness of the food source determines the rate at which digestion occurs and the consequent hunger state. For example, they taught young rainbow trout to bite at a red bar to obtain trout pellets. When the researchers halved the caloric content of the pellets by incorporating kaolin, a fine clay of no nutritional value, the fish emptied their guts twice as fast and attacked the food bar at twice the rate. Thus salmonids clearly can use internal receptors to monitor their nutrient intake and can adjust their feeding intensity accordingly.

My overall impression is that trout fairly bristle with information-gathering equipment: equipment sensitive to light, mechanical disturbance, chemicals, magnetic fields, temperature, acidity, salinity, and oxygen. At the same time the fish possess monitoring devices sensitive to such ingredients of their internal environment as endogenous rhythms, energy expenditure, and hunger state. After a brief discussion of natural selection theory, I will examine how trout use all this information in their daily lives.

Chapter 4

Perception

Imagine a late spring afternoon on Yellow Creek in south central Pennsylvania. Considerable numbers of mayflies are hovering over the river, but no trout are rising. Why? Could the lack of feeding activity be related to the cloudiness of the river after a recent spate of rain? On other days why do fish venture only so far from their holding station to retrieve drifting invertebrates? Or why do trout sometimes strike at so-called attractor patterns, gaudy concoctions of feather and fur far removed from the appearance of any natural food item? Or why will the fish occasionally react strongly to an elk-hair caddis of only a narrow size range, apparently ignoring both smaller and larger variants of the same pattern? In this chapter we explore a series of ideas and explanations in cognitive ecology that seem to bear on these questions. For some of these concepts we have little or no data from trout or salmon, so some of what follows will be a bit speculative, applying to trout some results that were obtained with other sorts of animals.

In chapter 1, I mentioned that rapid growth in trout should be the darling of natural selection because, in general, rapid growth should eventually result in more offspring produced per lifetime. Here I want to consider how a trout might think in order to promote the maximum growth rate possible under existing environmental conditions. I will emphasize here the decisions that trout make based primarily on rate of energy intake and, beginning in chapter 5, I will consider how energy acquisition by trout and their relatives can be compromised by responses to other factors such as risk of being caught by a predator (Dill 1987; Martel and Dill 1993, 1995).

We know that food energy taken in by a trout is partitioned into several activities, only one of which is growth. Now consider a trout that is holding its position in a stream, scanning the water ahead and to the side for drifting prey. The trout's problem, posed by natural selection, is how to behave in such a way as to garner the maximum amount of energy for growth. How might the trout do this?

Natural selection is focused on *net* energy intake because that is the rate most closely tied to growth rate. Net energy intake may be calculated at several levels, from ingestion of food to absorption across the gut wall. We will approach the matter by considering net energy intake to be the rate at which energy is consumed in the form of prey, less the energy expended in feeding. Students of animal feeding behavior think of the energy taken in as the benefit of feeding and the energy expended as the cost of feeding.

Let us start with costs. We know that as the current increases, trout expend more energy to hold a feeding station. Figure 4.1 shows graphically how such an energy cost increases with current speed (Hill and Grossman 1993). The exact location and shape of the cost curve will vary with the age and species of the trout or salmon (and with stream temperature, as we will see later on), but the important point is that a trout has to expend more energy to remain in a holding position in a stronger current.

Now for the benefits, a somewhat more complicated matter. Imagine that as current speed increases, potential food items drift more quickly past a station-holding trout, so the benefits of holding in faster water should be substantial. However, at some point the current becomes so rapid that a trout does not have enough time to detect, pursue, capture, and eat a prey item before many other items have swept past. So the benefit curve is humpbacked, with some intermediate current speed that potentially furnishes the trout with the greatest rate of energy intake (most prey) per unit of time spent foraging. Figure 4.1 portrays both the cost curve and the benefit curve in joules per hour. From examining just the benefit curve, one might conclude that the best policy for a trout would be to always hold station in water passing at about 45 cm per second, because that current speed results in the greatest rate of food intake. However, natural selection is not interested in just the benefit curve, which measures gross energy intake. Instead, natural selection most favors trout that have the greatest rate of net energy intake, the energetic benefits minus the energetic costs. So we look

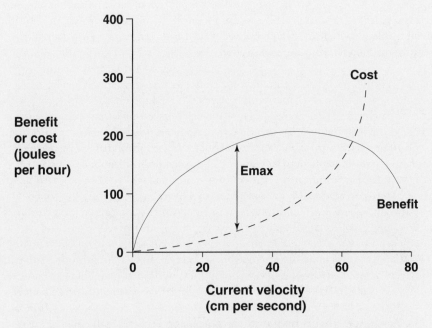

Figure 4.1. Current Velocity and Drift-Feeding Trout. This graph addresses the current velocity at which foraging trout should choose to hold station. Optimality theory focuses on the point at which the energy benefits of a behavior exceed to the greatest extent the costs of that behavior. Here both the benefits and costs vary with current velocity. The optimal current velocity is not where the gross rate of energy income from food is the greatest but where the net energy income—the difference between gross benefit and cost (Emax)—is highest. Thus the optimal current speed in this hypothetical example is 30 cm per second. (After Hill and Grossman 1993)

at figure 4.1 to determine the current speed that corresponds to the greatest result when energetic cost is subtracted from energetic benefit. The greatest net energy return occurs at a current speed of 30 cm per second.

This is what behavioral ecologists call *optimality theory.* We have predicted from knowledge of costs and benefits how an animal should behave to maximize its fitness. The theory says that natural selection should favor such behavior because no alternative would confer greater lifetime reproductive success. The important point from the perspective of this book is that the theory expects that a trout will avoid feeding at the highest possible rate. Instead, the theory expects the trout to discount energy input by how much it costs to obtain that energy. Thus in figure 4.1 the theory expects a trout to take in only about 200 J of gross energy per hour rather than the 225 J per hour that it could take in if it remained in a faster current.

We can imagine natural selection's favoring any behavior that would increase net energy intake by lowering the cost curve, raising the benefit curve, or both. For example, it is well known that trout often hold station in a reduced current flow that is near faster currents. A familiar example is the fish's lowering its cost curve by sheltering behind a midstream boulder while scanning the faster currents above and on either side.

Recent studies of Arctic grayling have added a complication to this optimal foraging theory (Hughes 1998). Imagine that along an Alaskan river, water temperature increases with distance from origin to mouth, certainly a common feature of streams fed by snowmelt. Now imagine a grayling that can take up station anywhere along that river. We have seen that at any particular location the fish should maximize its ratio of energy input to swimming cost, but how might it optimize its response to the temperature gradient? Hughes posited that if a grayling could get all the food it required and if its growth rate was therefore limited only by its digestive rate, it should live in the warmest water available (within tolerable limits) to maximize digestion rate. However, if such a fish could not get all the food it required, its growth rate would not be limited by its digestion rate but by the overall cost of metabolism. Thus a food-limited grayling should live in the coolest water possible to reduce its metabolic cost and maximize its growth rate. Hughes elaborated on these points by showing how trade-offs among various rates of energy intake, digestion, and metabolism predict where along a river the optimal habitat for a grayling would be expected to occur.

One factor that affects the mental processes of trout is social interaction with other fish, both of the same and other species. I will return to this matter later, but it is important to mention it in conjunction with Hughes's 1998 study. In his observations in Alaska, Hughes noticed that often the largest grayling were farthest upstream, with smaller fish inhabiting larger downstream pools. This seemed odd because conventional wisdom has it that small fish live in smaller water than do larger members of the same species. As in most salmonid fishes, grayling exhibit a social dominance hierarchy based simply on the bullying benefits of larger size. A larger fish can chase a smaller fish from anywhere in a stream that the larger fish covets. Hughes combined the dominance behavior of grayling with his energetics calculations to explain the phenomenon of large fish upstream. Because of the selective forces that I discussed earlier, large fish, which can live wherever they want to, reside in cooler upstream segments if a river has little food and in the warmer downstream water if a river has abundant food. Smaller grayling do the best they can to follow the same policy. The result is an interesting reverse-size gradient in some streams, with the grayling getting progressively smaller (and more subject to bullying) with distance downstream. Perhaps such a distribution is more widespread than we think; it apparently also exists among brown trout in certain New Zealand streams (Hughes 1998). I should point out, however, that because this whole scenario is built solely on a series of correlations, it furnishes only weak inference. A controlled manipulative study would be most welcome. For example, the researcher could dribble plant food into a food-poor river, thereby increasing the plant life and the invertebrates that the grayling feed on. Compared to a control river, the biggest grayling in a fertilized river should be found in warmer water farther downstream.

Let us return to figure 4.1 for a moment. Much of the discussion of trout cognition to come will focus on E_{max}, the maximum rate of net energy intake. There is not much a fish can do about its cost curve, the energetic cost of swimming in a particular current speed, but its mental processes could influence how far from passing food it can remain in order to hold station in slower currents. Therefore, I will focus mostly on the height of the benefit curve and to a lesser extent on its shape. Natural selection should operate to raise the benefit curve above the cost curve to increase net energy intake. Why isn't the benefit curve higher? That is, why can't trout capture more food than they do at any given current speed? Conversely, how is the benefit curve maintained as high as it is? What sort of mental processing helps a trout to capture as much food as it does at any point on the current-velocity scale? We will begin the search for answers to these questions of fundamental importance to trout biology by considering the ability of salmonids to perceive their food as it drifts by. We will then turn to considering how what psychologists term *attention* bears on the benefit curve. Certainly, the ability to remember the attributes of a particular food type could raise the benefit curve by helping trout recognize and capture a higher percentage of food passing at any particular current speed. Therefore we also will review certain types of learning relevant to trout biology and the memory processes that enable the trout to learn.

Internal factors such as social dominance status and hunger state have been shown repeatedly to influence the mental processes of animals, so we also will discuss social and hunger effects in this consideration of trout thinking. Finally, just as the foraging behavior of trout represents a trade-off between costs and benefits, so does the size and function of the animals' entire mental apparatus.

The concept of perception is a bit slippery. When we say that an animal perceives something, we mean not only that it detects the presence of that something but that it also identifies it as belonging to some particular category. Thus for a trout to perceive a drifting stonefly larva, it must detect the presence of an object in its visual field and it must also be able to distinguish that object as a larva rather than, say, a twig or bit of algae passing by. How can we tell whether perception has occurred? When dealing with other humans (at least those who speak the same language), detecting perception is easy enough: we just ask. Do you hear that sound of 14 kHz entering your left ear from your headphones? Which way are the legs pointing on the E in the third line? Do you smell the onions?

Lacking a language in common with animals, we must use indirect means to find out what they can perceive. Three principle indirect methods are now in use (Shettleworth 1998). The first, the province of neurophysiologists, uses tiny electrodes to measure electrical impulses within cells. A neuron, or nerve cell, receives such pulses from its dendrites and sends them along to other cells via its axons. Axons and dendrites function as tiny electrical lines, each surrounded by a thin layer of electrical insulation in the form of fat. The fat layer keeps messages from being confused by impulses jumping among dendrites or axons. The usual procedure in neurophysiological studies is to anesthetize an animal so that its sensory systems continue to function while it is unconscious. A stimulus of some sort is then presented to a sensory organ, and the researchers look for impulse traffic in the nerve-cell axons that link that organ to the brain. Much of our knowledge of stimulus detection by salmonid eyes, for example, has been determined using such techniques.

While electrophysiology can tell us the sort of information that the brain is receiving, other methods are required if we are to know what portion of such impulses is processed in the central nervous system and then acted upon by an animal. Of the whole-animal methods, the first investigates how naturally occurring behavior changes in response to natural or artificially manipulated stimuli. Much work with trout perception, some of it quite elegant, has used this technique.

The final approach to the study of perception capitalizes on an animal's ability to change its behavior with experience, that is, to learn things. Functionally, this approach simply uses means other than a common language to get animals to tell us whether they have perceived something in their environment. The formal name for this specialty is *psychophysics*, because it uses physical measurements of environmental stimuli and psychological measurements of animals' behavioral responses to such stimuli. I discuss most types of learning in a later section, so one example from salmonids of how psychophysics uses operant conditioning techniques will suffice here. The researchers were asking whether trout are sensitive to changes in the earth's magnetic field. In prospecting for an answer, they first closely monitored the behavior of captive rainbow trout. Every time a trout would happen to bump against a certain metal bar positioned in the aquarium, the observers would introduce food. The trout then gradually formed a mental association between bumping the bar and the advent of food, so the frequency of bar bumping increased through time. Once such an association had been formed, the researchers linked bar bumping to disturbance of the earth's magnetic force field. If bumping the bar was rewarded only when the magnetic field around the bar had been disturbed, trout eventually learned to bump the bar under those conditions. Thus the learned behavior demonstrated that the fish could detect the magnetic field. Although not a part of this particular experiment, pairing of operant response with manipulated stimulus has been widely used to explore thresholds of sensitivity of animals to various environmental stimuli, the conceptual equivalent of hearing or vision tests for humans.

With this short introduction concerning techniques for studying perception, I now turn to signal detection theory, a variety of cognitive ecology that bears directly on the benefit curve in figure 4.1. Imagine a rainbow trout that is holding station in northern Colorado's Cache la Poudre River. As the fish gently fins against the current, thousands of objects pass it in the drift. The fish immediately identifies some objects as food items suitable for pursuit and captures them during brief round-trips from its holding station. It immediately identifies other objects as nonfood, a category that might include twigs, fallen leaves, bits of algae, molted crayfish exoskeletons, and the like. Such nonfood items fail to elicit any stirring in the trout. Now the interesting questions are these. How does the trout decide what is food and what is not food? Is it always certain, or are there circumstances when it is uncertain? If it is uncertain, how does it decide to go check anyway, even though doing so raises its cost curve by the extra energy required? Signal detection theory provides a way to approach these questions.

But first we must digress. At the level of mental processing, signal-detection theory assumes that the trout sometimes doubts whether something going by is food. In contrast, a prominent bit of theory in the field of behavioral ecology is built entirely on the assumption that a trout never has such doubts. The theory is called *optimal diet selection theory,* and the assumption is that foragers have perfect knowledge about their food (Charnov 1976). Optimal diet selection and its perfect-knowledge assumption have greatly helped us to understand how animals forage, so they deserve discussion before we move on to signal detection.

Imagine that the Cache la Poudre trout is holding amid an entire constellation of passing prey items of different types. Perhaps some are mayfly larvae, some are grasshoppers on the surface, some are emerging midges. Optimal diet selection theory assumes that the trout has perfect knowledge of the energy content of each prey type. Now imagine that all these prey types are drifting by at various distances from the trout so that it must spend differing amounts of time and energy to secure each item and return to its holding station. The time required to capture and eat each identified food item is called *handling time,* and the time spent holding station while scanning the passing water for food is called *search time.* Thus, while feeding, a trout's time must be devoted to either search time for prey or handling time for detected prey.

The theory assumes that for every prey item going by, the trout knows the ratio of the energy in that prey to the time or energy cost of catching and eating it. If time is under consideration, every prey type is considered to have an E/h ratio (that is, a ratio of energy content to handling time) of, say, joules per second of required catching and eating time. If energy cost rather than time is in the denominator, the units of measurement become simply those of net energy, joules, for example. Remember that the theory says that the E/h ratio for each item drifting by is a function of both the number of joules in that item and the time or energy required to swim out, get it, return to station, and eat it.

According to the theory, a trout will have the highest net benefit curve (see figure 4.2) if it adheres to the following policy. First, it should rank mentally all passing food items according to their E/h (or net energy) content. Thus big energy-rich prey items such as salmon flies passing near the trout should be ranked the highest, and small energy-poor items like small ants passing at a distance should be ranked lowest. Large items far away and small items close by should be given intermediate ranks. Now things get a bit complicated. Imagine that a hatch of big energy-rich items like salmon flies results in enormous numbers of high E/h items drifting by close to the trout. Because these rich items are numerous, the trout's searching time is essentially zero because every time it finishes handling one salmon fly, the next is right there, ready to be captured. In such a case the optimal policy will be to ignore all other passing food types and concentrate only on the highly abundant, highest E/h food, the salmon flies in this example. Why? Because if a trout spends handling time in taking a lower-ranked item, it gives up search time for the highest-ranked food type. It is better to wait just for the energy-rich items. But remember that while the trout is waiting for salmon flies, it is ignoring lots of other passing food types.

Now suppose that time passes, and fewer and fewer salmon flies drift by. At some point in the diminishing parade of the highest E/h items, the net benefit curve will be highest if the trout begins to incorporate into its diet the next-highest-ranking prey type in terms of E/h, or net energy. Why is this? The answer lies in a comparison of search time and handling time. As the best item becomes rarer, the amount of time spent searching for that one item becomes a larger and larger fraction of total foraging time. An animal that incorporates into its diet the second-ranked prey type now has two types of items to search for, so

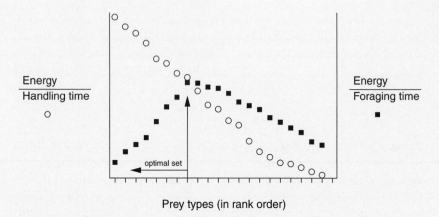

Prey types (in rank order)

Figure 4.2. How Should a Trout Decide What to Eat? Optimality theory focuses on the relation between number of different types of food in a diet and the overall rate of energy gain by an animal while foraging. Each open circle denotes a particular type of food item. According to optimal diet selection theory, the forager ranks the 21 different food types represented here according to their E/h ratios (the amount of energy in a food item [E] divided by the amount of time needed to catch and eat that item [h]). The line of circles descends from left to right, which shows that the forager has ranked these items according to E/h, with the highest-ranked item on the left and lowest-ranked item on the right. Thus the food item type with the most energy is not necessarily the highest-ranked item if it is also associated with a long handling time because then its E/h value might not be the highest.

Each open circle is associated with a filled square directly above or below it. The filled square symbolizes the forager's overall rate of energy gain (Energy/foraging time) during a foraging period if the forager catches and eats only those food types (open circles) at and to the left of the square. Note that the line of squares first rises and then falls as the fish adds increasing numbers of increasingly low-ranked prey to its diet. The theory says that some particular item in the array of diet items will produce the highest rate of energy gain if the fish eats only items of that E/h rank or higher and ignores all lower-ranked items. The vertical arrow shows this point. The complex of prey types to the left of the vertical arrow is the optimal set because it will provide the forager with the highest rate of energy gain possible. The line of squares eventually begins to decrease as the fish adds low-ranked items to its diet because of its need to strike a balance between handling time and search time. At some point a forager would be better off not investing handling time in catching and eating a low-ranked item and instead should use that time to search for high-ranked items. (After Charnov 1976)

its search time per item is reduced. If the handling cost of taking the second-ranked E/h item is more than recompensed by the reduction in search time, the fish should add it to its diet. The upshot of this approach is that an animal with perfect knowledge of the value, abundance, and distribution of all potential food types should incorporate only as many of those food types into its diet as will make its overall benefit curve of net energy the maximum possible. Because such a policy promotes the highest possible net energy intake, it is called optimal diet selection (figure 4.2).

Optimal diet theory has been tested with salmonids under carefully controlled conditions (Ringler 1979; Bannon and Ringler 1986), and the results have been equivocal. The reasons that the test results have not completely supported the theory are instructive for the student of trout thinking, so some data are worth examining in detail. Ringler (1979) examined optimal diet selection in brown trout confined to an artificial stream. In a series of trials he presented individual fish with a smorgasbord of prey types differing in E/h. The brine shrimp each contained 15 J, whereas large and small crickets contained 239 and 103 J, respectively, and large and small mealworms contained 230 and 105 J, respectively. Because in the test system the handling times for all these prey types were about the same, optimal diet theory would rank the prey types in a trout's diet as large crickets or large mealworms > small crickets or small mealworms > brine shrimp. The water in the artificial stream was extremely clear, light intensity approximated that of natural daylight, and no prey item drifted by more than about 25 cm away from a fish holding station. Thus we can assume that the trout could detect every food item.

Each trout was started out on a diet consisting of brine shrimp only. After it was taking these with regularity, Ringler added various combinations of large and small mealworms and large and small crickets to the shrimp in the drift. Suppose a fish was started out on brine shrimp, then had added to the drift large mealworms and small crickets. Optimality theory would say that, assuming the number of mealworms was sufficient, the trout should ignore the crickets and brine shrimp. If the supply of mealworms was inadequate, the fish should add the crickets but still ignore the brine shrimp.

In placing small crickets and large mealworms in the drift, Ringler used three ratios of small crickets to large mealworms, 1:1, 2:1, and 5:1. In practice, 34 brine shrimp were drifted by a trout per minute, while the combined numbers of small crickets and large mealworms passing the trout in any of the three ratios always totaled 10 per minute. Each trout was tested for 7 days after it had demonstrated a propensity to feed on brine shrimp in the system. On day 1 it received only brine shrimp, while on days 2 to 7 it received the same diet of shrimp, augmented with mealworms and crickets.

Because he knew the number of each of the three food types going by and the energy content of each item, Ringler could calculate the optimal foraging policy at each of the three ratios of small cricket to large mealworm, that is, the diet selection that would give the trout the highest benefit curve. He performed this calculation by counting the total number of prey items of all types consumed by a fish, then by assuming that if it was behaving optimally, a trout would take all large mealworms, then all small crickets, then as many brine shrimp as necessary until the total number of items of all food types equaled the observed total. Ringler also calculated the energy return if the trout had eaten the same total number of items but instead of being selective had consumed prey of the three types in proportion to their numbers in the drift.

Several aspects of the results, shown in figure 4.3, warrant attention. First, the somewhat irregular shape of each of the three lines in each of the three graphs reflects the fish's having eaten different total numbers of prey on different days. Second, the trout did not forage as well as optimal diet selection theory would predict. Even by day 7, none of the curves for observed consumption had reached the level of the curves for optimal consumption. Third, the animals clearly improved their performance. On day 1 they did no better than random consumption, that is, they were consuming the three types of prey in proportion to how often they saw them. The improvement of the observed curve with time means that the trout were letting increasing numbers of the low E/h brine shrimp, at least, go by. Ringler mentioned cases where trout even failed to respond to brine shrimp that were hitting them on the snout. Such a change in consumption pattern with time can only have been due to learning and memory.

When the fish had mealworms and crickets passing about once every 6 seconds, their consumption reached 65 to 78% of the best diet possible after 7 days. Look at what happened when the trout had to wait longer between mealworms and/or crickets. When these items were passing by only once every 12 seconds (the low drift rate in figure 4.4), the trout seemed to have trouble ignoring the low E/h brine shrimp. Of interest to the discussion of mental processes is that at the

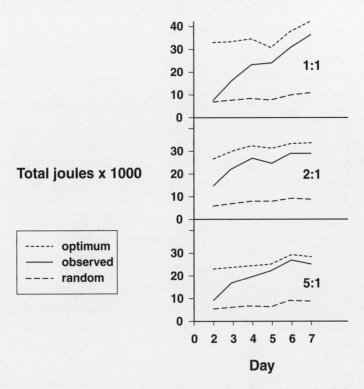

Total joules x 1000

optimum
observed
random

Figure 4.3. (opposite) Are Trout Optimal Foragers? This figure depicts the daily rate at which brown trout in an artificial stream obtained energy from food items drifted by them. In this example, meant to be a test of optimal foraging theory, the trout were presented with brine shrimp that had an energy content 15 J, large mealworms of 230 J, or small crickets of 103 J. The trout took about as much time to handle all three types of prey, so the researchers assumed that the trout were ranking their prey by energy content (that is, E) alone. In the example depicted, 34 brine shrimp were drifted by the trout per minute, while mealworms and crickets, combined, were drifted by at 10 per minute. The researchers varied the ratio of crickets to mealworms. In the top graph the ratio was 1 cricket for each mealworm; in the middle graph, 2 crickets per mealworm; and in the bottom graph, 5 crickets per mealworm. For a week the researchers calculated the amount of energy the fish took in each day, using knowledge of the numbers of the three types of items the trout ate during short observations.

The dotted line represents the amount of energy that a trout could have taken in had it followed optimal diet theory perfectly. It would have eaten every mealworm and cricket and as many brine shrimp as necessary so that the number consumed of all three prey types equaled the number it was observed to consume each day. The dashed line in each graph represents the amount of energy a trout would have taken in had it chosen from the various food items at random. Random consumption in the top graph would mean that a trout ate equal amounts of mealworms and crickets and 3.4 times as many brine shrimp as mealworms and crickets combined.

The solid line in each graph denotes the observed energy intake rate. The trout gradually improved their performance rate during the study week but never achieved the optimal rate. (After Ringler 1979)

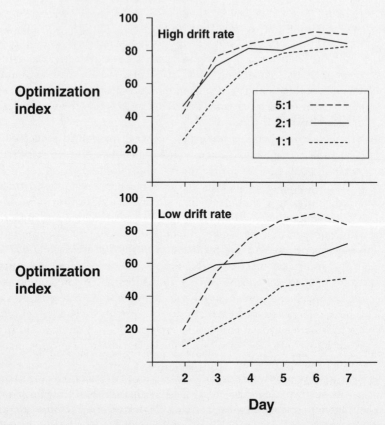

Figure 4.4. Calculated Optimization Indexes for Brown Trout. Each line represents the percentage of the maximum possible energy intake that the fish were observed to obtain from food items drifted to them in an artificial stream. For example, the dotted line in the upper graph is taken from the data in figure 4.3. A perfectly foraging trout would achieve an optimization index of 100. The five other lines here show that two factors involved in how closely a fish approached the optimal were the ratio of mealworms to crickets and the drift rate. In the upper graph twice as much food drifted by a fish per minute as in the lower graph. The fish improved their performance with experience but never reached perfection. (After Ringler 1979)

lower drift rate, the trout did quite well at the 5:1 ratio and much more poorly at the 1:1 ratio. At the 1:1 ratio neither mealworms nor crickets passed by frequently (only about 2.5 per minute for each type), while at the 5:1 ratio crickets passed by at about 4 per minute. It may have been difficult for trout to learn to respond when both the mealworms and the crickets drifted by infrequently.

Almost all the curves in figures 4.3 and 4.4 flatten out after 6 days or so, suggesting that under the conditions of the experiment, the animals would never have learned to do any better, no matter how many more days had passed by. Another result also points to limitations in trout cognition. The trout were wild natives caught in local streams where, presumably, they had never encountered brine shrimp. Ringler noted that in the lab it took 4 to 7 days for a fish to begin feeding on the shrimp and this in the total absence of any other food. Such gradual learning about an exotic food type is reminiscent of the ham-eating brook trout in the Grand Tetons and suggests that the fish were extremely conservative in their diet selection. One caveat needs to be added, however, and that is that the brine shrimp were dead and the fish were held initially in still-water aquaria. A much shorter lag time to first feeding on brine shrimp might have occurred had the shrimp been alive and swimming about or had dead shrimp been drifting past the fish in a stream.

To summarize this digression into optimal diet selection theory, even under excellent conditions for vision, trout feeding on prey types of different E/h value did not reach the theoretically maximal rate of energy intake. There was some indication that cognitive processes were responsible for the shortfall. After 5 or 6 days the trout's performance no longer improved. Furthermore, within a test session trout seemed to do better at a shortened time interval between exposures to items of the same prey type.

From Ringler's study it is clear that even under the most conducive conditions, trout did not catch prey as efficiently as they theoretically could have. Most problems for the trout in that study seem have been the result of imperfect learning abilities and memory. In short, we recognize that in the real world the assumption of perfect knowledge about prey types and distribution is never attained, so we are interested in what trout actually do know. This digression has been worthwhile because it underlines the importance of cognition for understanding trout biology.

To return to the thread of the main argument, the drift-feeding Cache la Poudre trout must decide at any given time whether some object is in its perceptual field and whether that object is food. If optimality theory is correct, it also must decide whether that detected food object is sufficiently energy rich to spend time and energy to obtain it.

The trout may be viewed as a receiver of signals, a receiver that associates certain categories of signals with responses (Wiley 1983, 1994). This pairing of reception and response has two levels. First, the fish must decide whether a signal (of any sort) is present or absent in the environment. Second, if it decides that a signal is present, it must decide whether it should respond to that signal. In both decisions signal detection theory holds that natural selection should produce fish that will respond or not respond according to a system of costs and benefits. So consider a trout that is not sure whether an object really is passing by at the edges of its vision or whether no object exists. Why is the fish unsure? Because the so-called signal-to-noise ratio for that object is very low. The distinction is low between the signal given off by the food item and the background sensory noise coming from the environment, in this case perhaps the scattering of light from small particles in the water or the mosaic of sunshine and shadow on the water surface. We also know from the discussion of vision that the ability of trout to detect a signal decreases toward evening.

The fish can make one of four responses to its perception. First, when the signal really is there, the fish can display what is known as a *correct detection* by swimming out, collecting the food item, and returning to its station. Second, the fish can fail to respond to a real object; this alternative is termed a *missed detection*. Third, the fish can make a mistake by swimming out after a perceived object that actually is not there at all, a response well termed a *false alarm*. Finally, the trout can correctly conclude that no signal exists and stay put. This last alternative is called a *correct rejection*.

Clearly, natural selection should favor trout that simultaneously have the highest chance of detecting a prey item when it is there (correct detection) and of not responding when a prey item is not there (correct rejection). As it turns out, it is impossible to maximize simultaneously both correct detections and correct rejections. For example, to maximize correct detections a trout would have to respond more often, but that would also lead to more false alarms. The theory says that natural selection should favor fish that maximize the ratio of correct detections to false alarms. How might this happen? Suppose that the horizontal axis in figure 4.5 represents some property such as brightness. The lefthand distribution, then, reflects variation in the under-

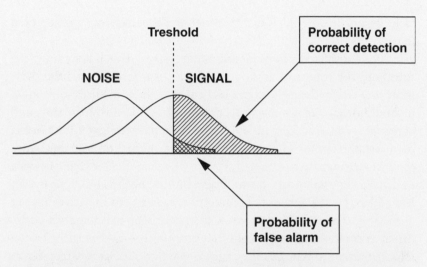

Figure 4.5. Signal Detection Theory. Assume that a trout is under selective pressure to be able to detect a particular signal against a background of sensory "noise," perhaps to be able to detect a mayfly larva drifting by against a background composed of duller hues. The graph shows that the brightness intensities of both signal and noise increase from left to right. Because the characteristics (such as brightness) of both the signal and the background noise vary from time to time and from place to place, a receiver such as a trout faces distributions of various brightness values for the signal and the noise, as the figure shows. The receiver is thought to select a particular response threshold of the signal or noise, such as intensity of brightness. If the receiver responds when the signal exceeds this threshold, the receiver is said to have made a correct detection. However, if the threshold is exceeded by the background noise and the receiver responds, the receiver has made a mistake and is said to have reacted to a false alarm. Note that in the figure, parts of both the signal distribution and the noise distribution exceed the brightness intensity value of the threshold (i.e., they are to the right of it). It is also possible for a receiver to respond mistakenly if there is no signal; this is called an incorrect detection. Finally, the receiver may fail to respond when only the background noise is present, an inaction termed a correct rejection. (After Wiley 1994)

water brightness of a stream, perhaps because of differing water depth, shadows from overhanging vegetation, and so on. The righthand distribution depicts the range of brightness values shown by a particular prey type, say, drifting mayfly nymphs. Now for the sake of argument suppose that the distribution of brightness of mayflies lies to the right of that for the environment, indicating that to a trout mayflies are on average brighter than their environment. However, the two distributions of brightness overlap. There is some range of values where the same brightness could indicate either the presence or absence of a mayfly.

Now consider the vertical line in figure 4.5. This line denotes the threshold for response. It says that if a trout perceives a brightness more intense (to the right of the vertical line) than the threshold value, it should behave as if a mayfly is there and should invest the time and energy to swim out from its holding station to investigate. Let's home in on the parts of the two curves to the right of the threshold line. Note that the area under the "mayfly" curve is much greater than the area under the "environment" curve. In general, as the threshold line moves left and right, the ratio of the mayfly curve area to the environment curve area changes. To summarize the underlying mathematics, natural selection should favor a trout that sets its response-threshold line in a location that maximizes the ratio of mayfly response (correct detection) to environment-only response (false alarm). Figure 4.6 illustrates this relationship.

Thus far we have been considering how a trout should respond to a food item versus the absence of a food item. Similar logic applies to choosing among different sorts of prey. In figure 4.5 the lefthand curve is meant to portray general underwater brightness. However, we can think of that curve as representing, say, the brightness of the lower E/h of two prey types or the brightness of nonprey items such as twigs. The trout's problem now is to perceive the difference in brightness between the two prey types or between a prey type and a nonprey item. Once we start considering responses to two or more types of items available in the drift, a number of attributes come into play. A trout might increase the chances of a correct detection by using other cues, such as color or texture.

Figures 4.5 and 4.6 are based on the assumption that the characteristics of the signal are somehow displaced from those of the noise so that signal and noise can be separated on the basis of a detection threshold. But suppose the signal is superimposed on the noise, such as might happen if a trout is to feed exclusively on one particular prey item of intermediate brightness. In such cases, according to the theory, there should be some optimal filter or tuned response, rather than a threshold. In practice such a filter is simply the region between an upper and a lower threshold. The same logic applies; natural selection

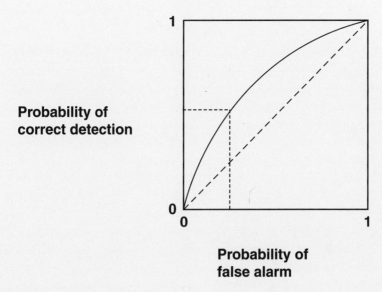

**Probability of
correct detection**

**Probability of
false alarm**

Figure 4.6. Maximizing Correct Detections. In signal detection theory the curve depicted by the convex solid line is called the receiver-operating characteristic. The location on the convex line marked by the intersection of the vertical and horizontal dotted lines corresponds to the threshold value in figure 4.5. The probability of a correct detection, which corresponds to the single-hatched area of the signal curve in figure 4.5, is marked by the corresponding value on the vertical axis in this figure. Similarly, the probability of a false alarm, which corresponds to the double-hatched area of the noise curve in figure 4.5, is marked by the corresponding value on the horizontal axis of this figure. The more widely separated the distributions for the signal and noise curves become, the more convex will be the curve of the receiver-operating characteristic. And the more convex the curve, the higher is the chance of a correct detection compared to the chance of a false alarm. Natural selection appears to have favored mechanisms that allow trout to increase the convexity of the curve. (After Wiley 1994)

should set the width of the filter (the distance between W and W′ or between N and N′ in figure 4.7) to promote the greatest possible difference on the receiver-operating curve (figure 4.6) between the chances of correct detection and false alarm.

We can expect many, if not all, of the sensory systems discussed in chapter 2 to be involved in signal detection. Natural selection should favor sensory thresholds or filters based on a prey item's size, hue, mechanical disturbance, or odor, as well as on its brightness.

How sensitive might a trout's filters be? The answer depends on the sensory system and on the form of the signal and noise. Odor

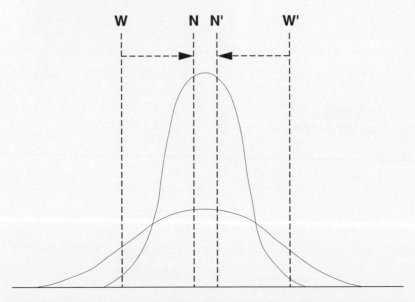

Figure 4.7. Signal Detection Theory: Substituting the Detection Window. Figure 4.5 advanced the notion that a trout might have a detection threshold that separates a characteristic of a signal, such as the brightness of a mayfly larva, from background "noise." The threshold was unidirectional in the sense that any value to the right of the threshold was more likely to correspond to the signal than to the noise. Signal detection theory also applies to bidirectional sensory filters. In this figure the signal holds an intermediate position within the distribution of characteristics of the sensory noise. For example, the signal might emanate from mayfly larvae of a limited size range within the size range of all items drifting past, both food and debris. We can think of such a filter as a range of values bounded by upper and lower thresholds. Note that as the refinement of the filter improves, that is, as the window narrows from W-W' to N-N', the chance of a correct detection becomes increasingly great relative to the chance of a false alarm. In figure 4.6 this means that as the width of a filter diminishes, the curve of the receiver-operating characteristic becomes more convex. In other words, if a trout can narrow the width of the filter that it is using to identify some particular prey type, the chance of a correct detection increases relative to the chance of a false alarm. (After Wiley 1994)

molecules can be thought of as digital (i.e., discontinuous) signals. There are discrete differences among odor molecules based on the identity, number, and position of their atoms. Natural selection has fashioned the olfactory sense in trout to separate signal and noise based on extremely small discrete differences in molecular structure. Analog (i.e., continuous) signals appear to present a more complex evolutionary problem for sensory systems and the perception that they serve. Here, signal and noise, or two different signals, can gradually blend into each other; there is no sharp line of demarcation. A general principle of perception, Weber's Law (Shettleworth 1998), has interesting implications for perception in trout. According to optimal foraging theory, trout should select prey items based on their ratio of energy to handling time, and energy content is usually a function of prey size. Weber's Law comes into play if we ask how good trout might be at distinguishing prey of different size; how refined could their diet selection be, based simply on perceptual ability? Weber's Law says that the just noticeable difference between two stimuli is a constant fraction, a quantity termed the *Weber fraction*. No one knows anything about how well Weber's Law might apply to trout, so we must rely on a theoretical example. Mayfly nymphs of 6 mm and 8 mm differ in length by 25%. According to Weber's Law, if this is the smallest difference between small mayfly nymphs that a trout can detect, 25% is the just noticeable difference between any two prey lengths. That is, Weber's Law predicts that such a trout would not be able to perceive the difference between 25-mm and 30-mm grasshoppers because the size difference (17%) is less than 25%. If trout do follow Weber's Law, they would be limited in how finely they could discriminate prey according to the ratio of energy to handling time. From the perspective of the angler, knowing something about the Weber fraction in regard to size might reveal, for example, how closely the hatch need be matched. Weber's Law is thought to hold for all detectable characteristics of a signal, such as brightness, hue, intensity, and amplitude.

The early application of signal detection theory to the behavior of animals focused on communication between one animal, the signaler, and a second animal, the receiver (Wiley 1994). Rather elaborate ideas were developed about the characteristics of signals designed by natural selection either to be maximally detectable against background noise or to deceive the receiver. I will defer discussion of maximally detectable signals to a later section in which I develop ideas about specific search images, but the notion of deceptive signals is quite interesting to pursue here in the context of communication between angler (signaler) and trout (receiver).

In certain cases natural selection should favor animals that send a signal disadvantageous to the receiver. These deceptive signals have been selected to maximize the probability of a false alarm reaction by a receiver. Such signals mimic another signal (the model signal) that normally elicits a correct detection. They are parasitic signals. For example, Krebs (1977) has put forward what he termed the Beau Geste hypothesis to explain why certain birds have a number of different song types in their vocal repertoire. (The hypothesis was named for the French Legionnaire who would prop up casualties, rifles in hand, to deceive attackers about the number of remaining defenders.) By singing different songs at different places in his territory, such a bird might deceive a receiver of the signals into concluding that more than one territory holder is already occupying the area, causing the receiver to move on in search of a territory elsewhere.

A second example of deception in animal communication concerns the remarkable signaling of femmes fatales fireflies (Lloyd 1965). As a rule, firefly males and females find each other for mating by signaling with their light organ. Males in flight signal with a species-specific pattern of flashes, a sort of arthropodal Morse code, and the flightless females respond to the males' signal with their own species-specific light signal. In this fashion males home in on and copulate with females of the proper species. Females of certain species in the firefly genus *Photuris* have evolved the capacity to deceive males of other species by mimicking the signals of their females. In response to the deceptive *Photuris* signal, males of the host species, adapted to home in for copulation, in fact home in to their deaths as they are killed and eaten by the, literally, femmes fatales.

Now what is an angler doing when "matching the hatch" besides sending a deceptive signal? The objective is to slip past a trout's sensory threshold (figure 4.5) or sensory filter (figure 4.7) and induce a false-alarm prey capture response. (I will discuss in chapter 5 why trout sometimes have narrow sensory filters that are difficult to pass.)

Before considering how various attributes of the environment affect signal detection in trout, it will be useful to lay out clearly the logic of why signal detection is important. Early on we saw that natural selection should generally favor trout that grow quickly. We then moved from the ecological level (monitoring growth) to the behavioral level. Fastest growth should be attained by trout that behave to obtain the most energy in their food for each unit of time or energy expended in obtaining that food. Hughes's work with grayling (1998) followed the same optimality argument, bringing water temperature into the picture as a factor mitigating reduced food abundance. Finally, signal detection is important because of its realism. Trout do not have perfect knowledge of their food supply. They cannot tell food from nonfood without error or high-efficiency food from low-efficiency food without making mistakes. In short, signal detection theory focuses on the best a trout can do, given less-than-ideal circumstances, to maximize its net energy intake and therefore its growth rate. Signal detection is important to the biology of trout. A major theme that I develop later in the book is the various ways that natural selection has equipped trout to separate signal and noise. Figures 4.5, 4.6, and 4.7 should be of continuing help in understanding the influence of such factors as attention, learning, and memory.

Although not couched in terms of signal detection theory, several recent experimental studies have explored how ambient light intensity, current speed, suspended debris, and water turbidity all reduce the so-called reactive distance of drift-feeding trout. We can interpret these studies as exploring how environmental factors increase the overlap between the distributions of noise and signal, making it more difficult for a fish to make correct detections and avoid false alarms.

As part of a comprehensive research program on the biology of Scottish Atlantic salmon, Neil Metcalfe and his colleagues (1997) have explored the responses of stream-feeding salmon parr to reductions in ambient light intensity. The main argument tested had two components. First, at night salmon should be less able to detect drifting prey as light intensity decreases; this argument is congruent with the anatomy and physiology of the salmonid eye (chapter 2). Second, the ability to detect prey in low light conditions should lessen with increased current speed because at substantial distances it should be less easy to detect prey passing by quickly. Considering the combined effects of current speed and light intensity, the salmon should have least difficulty detecting slowly drifting prey in higher intensities of light and most difficulty detecting rapidly drifting prey in dimmer light. The researchers predicted that natural selection should have fashioned salmon that would move into slower currents as the light became dimmer, thus reducing the number of prey that might drift by undetected. Although not applied in the Metcalfe study as an underlying concept, signal detection theory would say that by selecting slower water in lower light the fish would be acting to minimize missed detections.

Metcalfe and colleagues tested these ideas in an artificial stream, first by examining how much pelleted food salmon parr ate during a limited time period under various combinations of light intensity and water current. Then the fish were asked to select a current speed in which to forage at high and low light intensities. Metcalfe and his team varied light intensity over nine levels, from zero lux, meaning absolute darkness, to 300 lux, the condition shortly before dawn (1 lux = 0.1 foot-candle). The speed of the current was either 5 or 24 cm per second.

So long as they had adequate light by which to detect food, the fish caught as many pellets in the fast current as in the slow current. However, once the light fell below 1 lux, about the light intensity on a clear night of full moon, the capture rate at the high current speed fell off compared to that at the slower current.

Of considerable interest to anglers, the salmon compensated for lower light by moving into slower water. That is, as predicted, their overall rate of food capture was higher under conditions where they could see individual food particles better, even if fewer of those particles flowed past them per unit of time. The researchers elicited this response from the salmon by cleverly modifying the artificial stream. While the amount of water flowing through the entire system was kept constant, the side walls of the observation chamber were gradually tapered toward each other so that the farther downstream a fish took up station, the faster the current flowing by would be.

Low light intensities caused the young salmon to choose the slower current upstream in the chamber (figure 4.8). In terms of signal detection theory, such behavior might have served to separate better the distribution of the signal (food pellet) from the distribution of the noise (walls of the artificial stream), thus increasing the likelihood of correct detections and decreasing the likelihood of false alarms.

The researchers must be chided, gently, for testing the parr in groups of 15 animals rather than as singletons. As I will discuss later, an important constraint preventing some fish in a school from foraging optimally is the despotic social behavior of other nearby fish. In the

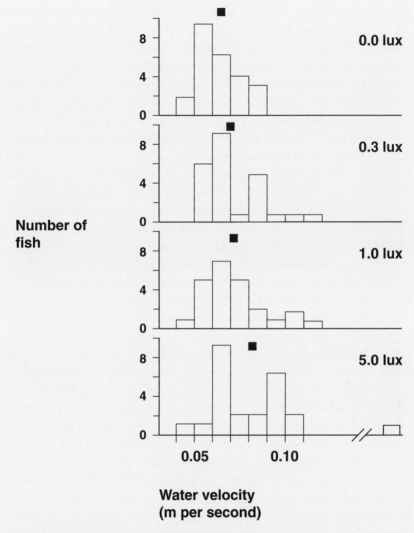

Figure 4.8. Holding in Slower Current in Lower Light. This graph shows the influence of ambient light intensity on the water velocity chosen by station-holding drift-feeding juvenile Atlantic salmon. Extremely low light intensities markedly decrease a trout's visual acuity. As signal detection theory anticipates, the fish chose to stay in slower and slower currents as the light intensity decreased, presumably to increase the probability of correct detections of food items drifting by. (After Metcalfe et al. 1997)

Metcalfe experiment the behavior of dominant conspecifics may have prevented some fish from locating at their first-choice position in the stream. Interference such as this could explain the spread of values at each light intensity in figure 4.8. I would really like to know what the fish would have done if tested singly, when they would have been truly independent of each other in their responses. Would they all have selected the slow end of the water-current distribution at each of the four light intensities? Nevertheless, this study clearly demonstrated that fish compared their detection rates under the feeding handicap of low light intensities and used that information to elevate capture rates under the circumstances. As Metcalfe and his coworkers pointed out, previous findings that steelhead (Edmundson et al. 1968), brown trout (Heggenes et al. 1993), and rainbow trout (Hill and Grossman 1993) moved into slower water at night could have resulted from the fish's maximizing their feeding rates under low light levels.

Very low light intensities apparently exert differing degrees of influence across salmonids. One study determined that at very low light intensities, Dolly Varden char could detect prey at greater distance than could cutthroat trout (Henderson 1982). Although this work was performed with fish cruising for prey in still water, we might expect the same distinction between drift-feeding animals of the two species. Study of species-typical rods and cones in the retina provided an anatomical basis for the difference in behavior between the two species.

Turbidity is another factor that reduces the distinction between signal and background noise. Artificial channels created within an existing stream and containing various concentrations of suspended sediment have been used to examine rainbow trout feeding in water made increasingly cloudy (Barrett et al. 1992). While certainly an indication of the degree of cloudiness or murkiness of water, turbidity is defined technically as the quantity of light absorbed or scattered by a sample of water and is evaluated with several different types of units, one of which is the nephelometric turbidity unit (NTU). In the rainbow trout study, while ambient stream water measured between 4 and 6 on the NTU scale, fish were also asked to forage in more turbid water, of either 15 or 30 NTU, produced by adding silt, sand, and fine organic matter.

Wild-caught rainbow trout were tested singly for their reaction distance to mealworm pieces allowed to drift by. Increased turbidity had an effect similar to that of decreased light intensity at night: the trout detected only closer prey as the water became cloudy (figure 4.9). At the highest level of turbidity the fish appeared to detect prey only half as far away from themselves as they did under conditions of normal stream clarity. Turbidity had no effect on pursuit speed, so that once the decision had been made to take a passing item, the fish were equally aggressive in apprehending it from the drift. Incidentally, the oft-heard notion that trout in turbid water notice black wet flies more than light-colored ones can be tested by using the methods proposed in appendix 1.

As applied to feeding trout, the "noise" in signal detection theory may be either from general background clutter or from nonfood objects that the trout confused with the signal. In the salmon parr and rainbow trout projects that I have just discussed, presumably the fish encountered increased difficulty in detecting food against background clutter as light intensity lessened or turbidity increased and thus displayed a shorter and shorter reaction distance. A complementary investigation of feeding behavior in Arctic grayling focused on the effect of drifting debris on feeding responses to current speed (O'Brien and Showalter 1993).

O'Brien and Showalter maintained grayling one at a time in an artificial stream and fed them a common freshwater crustacean, daphnia, that was added to the drift. An ingenious videotaping system allowed the researchers to monitor how far away each daphnia was when it first stimulated a reaction from a fish. The grayling project used faster current speeds than the salmon parr study and, at the higher current speeds (46 and 56 cm per second), found a decrease in detection distance. That is, at these quite fast currents, only daphnia passing rather close to a fish elicited a feeding response. However, up to a point, a trout can compensate for a smaller detection distance in faster currents by having access to more prey drifting by per unit of time. The interaction between detection distance and frequency of prey in the drift determines the encounter rate. In the grayling study the encounter rate with daphnia actually increased in current speeds up to 46 cm per second before falling off at higher current speeds.

Especially in the autumn, those fishing in streams bordered by deciduous forest are often inconvenienced by fallen leaves, twigs, and other debris in the drift. The grayling study demonstrated that such

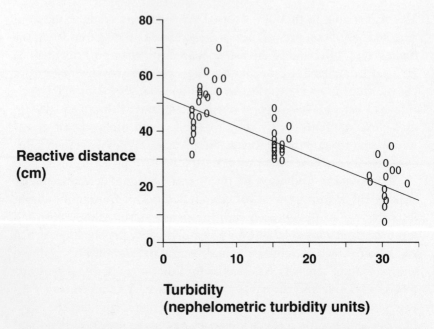

Figure 4.9. Turbidity and the Reactive Distance to Food. This graph shows the effect of water turbidity on the reactive distance to food items by rainbow trout that are drift feeding in artificial stream channels. In the parlance of signal detection theory, increasing turbidity reduced the distinction between the food items (signal) and the background (noise), so that only food items increasingly close to the fish were detectable. (After Barrett et al. 1992)

debris also hinders drift-feeding salmonids. Plant and detrital debris was drift-netted from a nearby river and then added to the test stream, where it cycled around and around in the system. Now the grayling had to detect a signal (daphnia) from among a great deal of inedible particulate noise.

The debris considerably reduced the ability of the fish to detect food, with both the angle and distance of their reaction to passing food decreasing (figure 4.10). Although it would be particularly interesting to know whether the deleterious effect of detritus became increasingly severe as current speed increased, the researchers did not present an analysis of such an interaction. One feature of this otherwise fine study presents a problem for students of trout cognition. Because of inadequate information about attributes of the detritus, it would be impos-

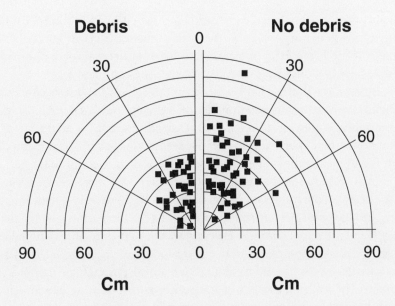

Figure 4.10. Debris and Reduced Signal Detection. This graph illustrates the role of debris in reducing signal detection by Arctic grayling that were holding station while feeding on prey drifting by in an artificial stream. The debris consisted of plant parts and detritus collected with a drift net from the water moving down a nearby river and then was added to the recirculating current in the experimental system. The researchers tested the ability of the grayling to detect individual daphnia (a small planktonic crustacean) added to the stream either with or without debris. To read the figure, imagine that a grayling is facing toward the top of the page with its eyes at the lower zero point. The lefthand and righthand quarter circles depict, respectively, the grayling's responses to daphnia in the presence and absence of debris. Each square represents the location where a fish leaving the lower zero point intercepted one drifting prey item. When the system was debris free, the fish detected daphnia at greater distance, both in front and to the side. In the lingo of signal detection theory, "noise" from debris increased the probability of a missed detection of a daphnia "signal." (O'Brien and Showalter 1993)

sible to replicate the work. This salmonid/detritus system offers some intriguing possibilities for examining signal detection theory, but before that can happen researchers need to considerably tighten up detritus management. Some detrital analogue of the nephelometric turbidity unit is a must.

We might imagine that trout could adjust their foraging positions in a stream in response to the amount of detrital noise. However, it is hard to imagine a stream in which detritus might vary in density from place to place, its having been mixed up thoroughly by turbulence during its downstream passage. Perhaps naturalistic observations could be made at the confluence of streams of different detrital load, although other factors would vary, as well, between the confluents.

It is evident that we have only bits and pieces of the puzzle concerning how various environmental factors influence perception. Considerable opportunities exist for examining together several or all the factors mentioned here, particularly because we now have statistical methods for teasing apart the influences of several co-varying conditions.

In an evolutionary sense, might potential prey species take advantage of such constraints on signal detection by trout as low light intensity, fast current speed, turbidity, and debris? In the parlance of the theory, we might expect natural selection to favor any attribute that makes prey resemble noise rather than a food-indicating signal, thus causing missed detections by feeding trout. For example, though the matter has apparently not been studied in any organized fashion, we can imagine drifting prey that mimic drifting detritus in color and texture.

In considering detectability of prey items by trout against background noise, it seems important to distinguish between prey that drift intentionally and prey that drift accidentally (Bader 1997). Although many stream invertebrates are accidentally dislodged or can release their hold on the substrate and enter the drift in response to disturbance, some species, such as those in the mayfly genus *Baetis*, intentionally enter the drift under nondisturbance circumstances. Studies have suggested that invertebrates might enter the drift voluntarily in response to low food supplies, intense competition for available food, local predators, or low oxygen. We might expect these intentional drifters to show the greatest adaptations fostering missed detections by trout.

One method that invertebrates could use to avoid detection would be to drift at night when light intensities might be too low for trout to see them. We have good evidence that the larvae of *Baetis* mayflies and other intentional drifters do drift mostly at night and, satisfyingly to the apostle of natural selection, that daytime drifting is more inhibited in the presence than in the absence of trout (Douglas et al. 1994; McIntosh and Peckarsky 1996). Douglas and his colleagues examined the temporal distribution of drifting mayflies over a 24-hour period in California streams with and without rainbow trout or any other drift-feeding fish species. Although trout presence appeared to have no effect on the numbers drifting at night, lower numbers drifted during the day in trout-occupied streams. Furthermore, the reduction in daytime drift occurred mostly within the larger size classes of nymphs. This latter result is what would be expected if larger nymphs were either more detectable or were differentially taken by trout because of their larger E/h ratios.

In a lovely field manipulation Douglas and his colleagues then nailed down the cause-and-effect relationship between trout presence and mayfly drift and demonstrated a mechanism that may account for the relationship. In each of several previously troutless streams, they placed two rainbow trout in a cage 15 m upstream from a drift-collecting net. Over a 3-day period they measured the numbers of mayflies entering the drift day and night by counting at dusk and dawn the nymphs caught in the net. Before and after this 3-day period, they set the same cage and net system in place, minus the trout. Records for the two troutless control periods were pooled for comparison with the 3 days when trout were present.

Adding the trout had no effect on the number of mayflies drifting at night but reduced the number drifting during the day by about 30%. McIntosh and Peckarsky (1996) obtained similar results in an artificial stream, for Colorado mayflies responding to water occupied by brook trout. Based on these results, it is difficult to fault the researchers' claim that mayflies react behaviorally to trout by detecting fish odor carried downstream. Such a reaction by the insects leads to the question of whether there might be a cognitive ecology of trout prey, a topic beyond the scope of this book. While it seems possible that stream-dwelling invertebrates might be more likely to enter the drift voluntarily in turbid water because of reduced detectability under such conditions, there appear to be no data on this point from adequately controlled studies.

Before leaving the topic of perception, I must mention one cautionary note. I have been viewing these various feeding trials from the perspective of signal detection and therefore have been using the terms *detection* and *detection distance* in describing trout behavior. It is only fair to point out that the authors of these projects are properly cautious by using the term *reaction distance* rather than *detection distance*. The difference in terminology is important. If a fish reacts to a passing object by swimming to it and eating it, we can have great confidence that it has detected that object. However, if a fish does not react to a passing food item, we cannot know whether it has detected that entity and rejected it (correct rejection) or failed to detect it (missed detection). The distinction between correct rejection and missed detection is almost impossible to make in naturally behaving animals and can be approached only by using the psychophysical techniques that I outlined earlier.

Finally, signal detection, like many other aspects of trout behavior, is profoundly affected by what are called *state variables*. State variables describe the current physiological or social condition of an animal, such measures as hunger state or social dominance position. For example, when a trout has to decide whether it should react to an item drifting past as if that item were food, how hungry the trout is should matter. After compiling other psychological ingredients of trout thinking, I will return to consider the influence of state variables.

Chapter 5

Attention

Imagine throwing and catching a Frisbee with a friend under some rather trying conditions. The wind is blowing directly from your friend to you, so the Frisbee usually approaches you from directly upwind. Because you are playing catch under a grove of oak trees on quite a blustery autumn afternoon, hundreds of leaves are blowing toward you along with the Frisbee. Keep this Frisbee game in mind as we consider how attention affects trout foraging.

We have seen how perception of food items among the drift appears to involve a trout's setting some mental threshold or filter to separate characteristics of the food signal from characteristics of nonfood "noise." If a trout had some mental capacity that made more distinct the characteristics of signal and noise, it might be able to increase correct detections and reduce false alarms, thus benefiting its net rate of energy income. The concept of selective attention, or just attention, has been proposed as one method for separating signal from noise.

Shettleworth (1998) defined attention as the mechanism for selecting what to respond to from moment to moment. Thus attention is clearly related to our everyday concept of concentration. "Stay focused on the game!" exhorts the ice hockey coach. Therefore, attention is a process of the central nervous system that differentially suppresses some stimuli coming from external and internal environments and emphasizes others. A good example is the subway rider intensely concentrating on her paperback in the corner of the car while ignoring the 50-decibel roar and screech of the wheels on the tracks.

Research on attention in both humans and pigeons has shown that the number of distractors affects the ability to detect a specified target. (The psychological term *distractor* is essentially equivalent to noise from other stimuli, and *target* is the same as signal.) Imagine that in your Frisbee game people are throwing five sizes of Frisbees to you and you are to catch only the largest. What mental processing might aid your task? If the target (signal) is quite different in appearance from the distractors (noise), the target is said to "pop out" in the mind of the receiver (Shettleworth 1998). Figure 5.1 illustrates a visual pop-out effect. It turns out that if the target is extremely distinctive, the number of different distractors has little or no bearing on the proportion of correct detections. Imagine in the Frisbee game that Frisbees of all sizes are painted the same color, perhaps to match the color of red oak leaves, except for the largest Frisbee, which is painted international orange. It is easy to appreciate that no matter how many Frisbees of different sizes were coming at you, the size you are searching for would still pop out.

It seems likely that mites "popped out" to brook trout foraging in Cement Creek, Colorado (Allan 1981). A comparison of the proportions of various food types in the trout's stomachs with the proportions of the same food types in the drift revealed that the fish were differentially taking the most abundant prey types and, in line with optimality theory, were concentrating more than at random on large items. However, the mites were an exception. Even though the mites were very small, the fish were taking them far out of proportion to their abundance in the drift. A pop-out effect seemed to be at work because the mites were bright orange or red and were found in the drift during the daylight hours. We know from chapter 2 that trout have good reception of red and orange wavelengths during daylight. Incidentally, we must also conclude that predation by stream-dwelling fish must be a negligible factor in the overall survivorship of these mites, or natural selection would not have them going around in such gaudy colors.

What are "attractor patterns" of artificial flies if not pop-out targets? Gaudy salmon flies, for example, are clearly not designed to mimic the appearance of any food type that a salmon would normally see. According to the theory, such a salmon fly is so detectable that it elicits a feeding response even when the number of distractors (natural food types) is large. Functionally, it is a feathered Cement Creek mite.

Psychological research has concentrated on visual pop-out targets, but chapter 2 contains examples of what may be pop-outs in other

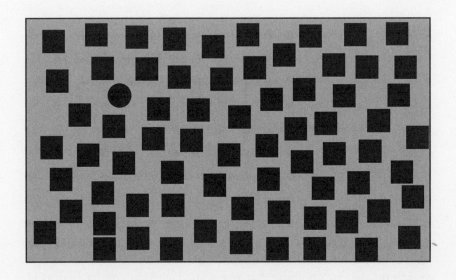

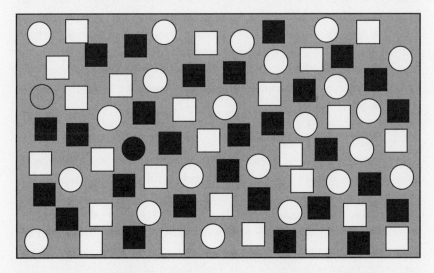

Figure 5.1. The Visual "Pop-out" Effect. Pop-out characteristics of a target enhance its detection. In the upper graph the single pop-out characteristic of shape makes finding the circle easy. In the lower graph a viewer must notice two characteristics, shape and color, to find a target, the black circle. Targets with more than one pop-out characteristic take longer to find. (After Shettleworth 1998)

sensory systems. The strong response to the chemical L-alanine or to sound wavelengths of 50 to 140 Hz may have been related to pop-out stimuli.

Remember the assumption of optimality theory about perfect knowledge? According to that assumption, a forager instantly recognizes all potential prey items and then captures only those item types that have E/h values large enough to be included in the optimal set. In the Frisbee game you now must catch only the three larger Frisbees (correct detections) and never touch either of the two smaller ones (correct rejections). From work with pigeons we know that this requirement makes things harder. Contrary to optimality theory, searching for several kinds of target at the same time slows the ability to detect any targets (figure 5.2).

Suppose that Frisbees of different sizes are coming at you at such a great rate that by the time you notice their size, many have already sailed past you. Could it be that if you concentrated on just one type of Frisbee, and caught all or almost all of them, you could do better even while letting other types go by? Concentrating on just one target type to the exclusion of all others has been called forming a specific search image. Specific search images were first invoked to explain some completely unexpected behavior by small birds, part of a story that merits a digression.

During the two world wars northwestern Europe experienced a timber famine. War machines were so hungry for wood products that many countries, among them The Netherlands, were stripped practically naked of forests. After the wars Europe undertook massive reforestation programs, in many cases substituting enormous plantations of fast-growing exotic conifers for the extirpated native deciduous hardwoods. Naturally, the various national forestry commissions were given the task of removing impediments to the growth of these young forests. The Netherlands employed Lucas Tinbergen to examine whether birds might have an effect on conifer-eating insects, mainly caterpillars. Many native songbirds were known to eat caterpillars and to feed them to their nestlings. The idea was that if such birds could be shown to act as a biological control agent, the forestry commissions would add great numbers of nest boxes to the young forests to increase avian populations. Although long-term nest box studies continue even today in a number of

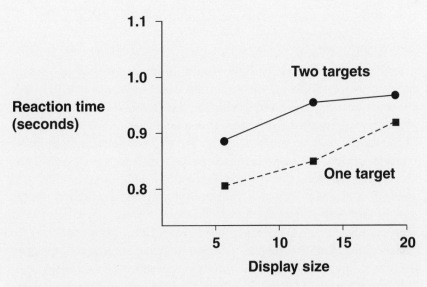

Figure 5.2. Locating Targets amid Many Distractors and Targets. This graph shows the effect of the number of distractors and targets on the ability of a pigeon to locate the targets. Whether the pigeon was trying to locate one or two targets, it took longer as the display size (the number of different types of distractor) increased from 5 to 20. Regardless of display size, it took the pigeon more time to find a target when it was simultaneously searching for two different types of target, rather than only one type. (After Blough 1989)

European countries, it now seems clear that avian predators cannot stop an outbreak of forest insect pests, although some researchers think that birds may have an effect when the insects are at low levels to begin with.

What does all this have to do with attention and specific search images? As part of their work, Tinbergen (1960) and his colleagues monitored every food item brought into a nest box by nestling-attending adults. Records were collected automatically by a flash camera that was triggered every time an adult bird brought food to its nestlings and stuck its head through the entrance hole of the nest box. A wristwatch mounted on the inside of the box facing the camera was used to record the time of each entry. In this way the researchers hoped to determine how many of each type of forest insect pest the parents were feeding to each brood of young. Then the researchers could use knowledge of the density of nests in the forest to calculate the extent of biological control by each bird species per hectare of forest. (One hectare is 10,000 m², or about 2.5 acres.)

In the course of his work Tinbergen found something totally unexpected, parent birds that were bringing caterpillar types in runs. Over a summer the various species of caterpillars hatched from eggs at different times and grew at different rates, so the variety of prey types available to the birds shifted with time. Tinbergen monitored the abundance of the various insects in the forest. When he compared relative abundance of a given insect type in the landscape to relative abundance of the same type in the food brought to nestlings, he found a distinct lag. Each caterpillar type would grow in numbers in the trees but would not be represented in the bird samples until well after it first appeared. Then, very quickly, it became a dominant item among the delivered food. Tinbergen concluded that this phenomenon stemmed from a psychological process that he termed the *specific searching image* or, nowadays, *specific search image*. The various caterpillars brought to the nestlings all had the property of being cryptic: they matched in color pattern the branches and needles on which they foraged. Tinbergen suggested that until caterpillars of a given type reached a considerable density, a foraging bird would not find them often enough for them to make a mental impression. That is, the bird would not remember what the caterpillars looked like well enough to focus on them. However, once a threshold encounter rate had been reached, a bird would begin to focus its attention on that one caterpillar type. It would form a mental representation, a specific search image, for that one type of caterpillar. In signal detection theory we might say that a specific search image has the same function as a pop-out characteristic of prey—it greatly increases the signal-to-noise ratio for that one prey item. Other prey types besides the one fostering the search image constitute part of the background noise; they are not even recognized as food. Note how different this idea is from optimal diet selection theory. According to search image theory, any particular type of food item not being taken is thought to be not detected at all by the predator, while, according to optimality theory, such an item is detected but is rejected as not in the optimal set.

In rural areas a popular pastime in the spring is quartering plowed fields to search for projectile points (arrowheads). Many hunters clearly develop a specific search image for the visual characteristics of flint and do not mentally register other forms of stone. Interestingly, the search image is very much focused on the texture of flint (much smoother that most other forms of rock or stone), rather than on its color, which can vary from coal black to the party colors of Ohio's famous "Flint Ridge" flint.

Would forming a search image for just one prey type allow a trout to gather more net energy per unit of time than attending simultaneously to items of several different sorts? Experimental evidence from other species suggests that it might. Pietrewicz and Kamil (1981) performed a series of experiments to test the function of specific search images in blue jays. Blue jays commonly eat moths in nature, and in one variation of the experiment Kamil's team asked captive jays to find cryptic moths. Ingeniously, the presentations were made by having the jays watch a slide show of moths and bark. In the actual task, if a blue jay pecked at a slide containing a picture of a camouflaged moth, a correct detection, it was rewarded with a mealworm (which blue jays love). If it refrained from pecking at a slide lacking a moth, a correct rejection, it was also given a mealworm. In practice the research used two types of moth on two types of background, and it certainly appeared that the birds used a specific search image to improve their performance (figure 5.3).

When a bird was shown a series of different pictures, one type of moth on one type of background, its percentage of correct detections improved faster than if the two types of moth and background were mixed. Also, seeing a run of slides of the same prey type improved the birds' ability to detect that prey type. Interestingly, runs of the same prey type and background also improved the jays' ability to make correct rejections, to avoid responding when a slide lacked any moth at all (Pietrewicz and Kamil 1981).

I have been unable to find any similar tests of specific search images in trout or salmon, yet the experiences of many anglers suggest that such a mental aid to foraging is widespread. Indeed, the whole notion of "matching the hatch" rests on the proposition that under many circumstances trout will feed on only one sort of prey type. Furthermore, it seems likely that such a specific search image for one prey type is formed only after that prey type has increased so much in density that a drift-feeding trout has been passed by dozens, hundreds, or

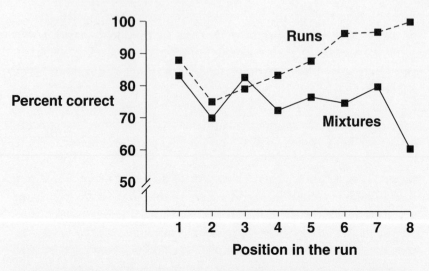

Figure 5.3. The Power of Imagination. The ability to detect a signal is improved by formation of a specific search image for that signal. Blue jays that viewed photographic slides of moths resting on matching backgrounds of bark provided evidence of the formation of specific search images. If a bird viewed a series of different slides of the same moth species, its percentage of correct responses improved during the run. However, if a bird saw a mixture of slides showing two cryptic moth species and two different matching backgrounds, its performance did not improve. The bird's memory for a particular moth type improved after seeing it a number of times in succession. (After Pietrewicz and Kamil 1981)

thousands of the "new" food type. In his study of brown trout diet selection Ringler (1979) mentioned that he sometimes had trouble inducing animals to begin feeding on brine shrimp, a novel prey type, even after several days.

Is there any way that natural selection might have fashioned insect prey to capitalize on the tendency of trout to form specific search images? The blue jay results suggest that trout prey types could behave in such a way as to discourage "runs" by feeding fish. When an intentional drifter leaves others of its own species on a substrate patch, could it be responding in a way that would lessen the chances that a trout would find enough prey of one type to form a search image?

Now let us consider how predation risk affects optimal foraging. Work during the 1990s showed that early optimality theory, such as described in figure 4.2, was a bit naive. It is not enough to consider growth or net energy intake alone as the object of natural selection. For example, an animal that forages in a way that promotes rapid growth rate loses if by doing so it is likely to be eaten by a predator. Currently, many researchers are proceeding under the assumption that natural selection favors activities that promote efficient feeding and rapid growth, discounted by activities promoting survivorship. Gilliam and Fraser (1987) put this idea succinctly in their assertion that animals should forage to minimize their "deaths per unit [of] energy." That is, an animal should consider both the chances of being killed by a predator and the net rate of energy income in deciding where, when, and how to look for food. Figure 5.4 suggests that for animals that could be killed by a predator while they are foraging, some best level of attention to food, rather than watching for potential predators, will give them the lowest chance of being killed by a predator for each unit of net energy obtained while foraging.

Elliot (1994) found that during their first winter, young brown trout in captivity simply did not eat, even in the presence of ad libitum food. Such a finding is explainable if, in nature, little food is available to these young fish in winter and their own predation risk then is so high that they are best off not eating and simply hiding in crevices for the winter.

Let us return to the imaginary Frisbee game amid the high winds and blowing leaves. Now imagine that people are playing baseball nearby and that every now and then a line drive comes screaming your way. Under such conditions you might have a strong tendency to devote some of your attention to the state of play in the ball game to reduce the chances of being hit in the head. Several recent projects suggest that trout similarly might divide their attention between obtaining their own food and keeping a lookout for predators. That is, as the theory in figure 5.4 predicts, they might not behave to garner the largest amount of net energy but to garner the largest amount of net energy per unit of predation risk.

Before proceeding further, it would be a good idea to be confident that animals concentrating on feeding rather than predators actually are more likely to be killed and eaten. While not yet demonstrated in salmonids, such a relationship has been shown in guppies. Guppies took longer to capture individual daphnia as the density of daphnia

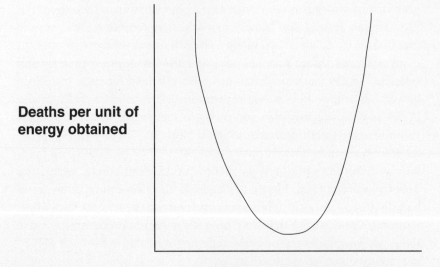

Deaths per unit of energy obtained

Proportion of attention to food rather than to predators

Figure 5.4. Eat or Get Eaten. A theoretical relationship exists between attention to food getting and attention to predator detection. Gilliam and Fraser (1987) suggested that natural selection should favor an animal that minimizes "deaths per unit of energy obtained" while foraging. In the figure, if an animal spends too little or too much time looking for food, it increases its chances of dying per unit of energy obtained. For any particular combination of food abundance and predator abundance, some value of attention to food should provide the lowest (i.e., optimal) ratio of deaths per unit energy required.

increased, presumably because it was harder to pick out just one daphnia to attack. At the same time guppies taking longer to catch daphnia were more likely to be killed and eaten by a cichlid used as a guppy predator. Godin and Smith (1988) concluded that because the guppies had to devote more of their attention to daphnia, those feeding on dense aggregations had less time to devote to scanning for their own predators and paid the price.

A fair amount of indirect evidence shows that trout and salmon sacrifice food getting in the presence of their own predators. For example, in an artificial stream brown trout used a riffle more, a pool habitat less, and consumed food items at a lower rate when a trout-eating pike was present than when it was absent (Greenberg et al.

1997). The prey, amphipod crustaceans, were found almost exclusively in the pools, where they were, in a sense, protected from the trout by the pike.

Domestication of salmonid fishes has been shown to reduce their adaptive responses to predators. Johnsson and Abrahams (1991) raised wild-type steelhead trout in the lab, along with hybrids of wild-type steelhead and domesticated rainbow trout. (Steelhead and rainbow trout are the same species.) When tested for their tendencies to feed close to an adult rainbow trout predator, hybrid juveniles did so more often than wild-type juveniles. The more risky behavior of the partially domesticated fish might not have caused greater mortality if the domestics were better able to avoid being caught by the trout predator. Such was not the case, however, as fish of both types were equally likely to be caught.

I should point out that the nature of the experiment leaves some doubt about the actual behavioral mechanism involved in the response difference between the two types of fish. In each replicate of the project 10 wild-type and 10 hybrid fish were tested together. It is known that domesticated salmonids tend to be more aggressive than their wild progenitors (Moyle 1969; Swain and Riddell 1990), so the hybrids could have excluded the wild-type fish from the risky feeding site rather than the latter's avoiding it on their own. It would have been preferable to test each genetic type separately and ideal to test one fish at a time. In any case the apparent reduction in wariness of the domesticated fish suggests that interbreeding between released or escaped domestic strains and natives could increase rates of depredation on formerly completely wild stocks.

Common mergansers are fish-eating ducks that can have a substantial effect on the numbers of trout and salmon. The birds scan for their fish prey mostly by peering about with their heads under water while swimming on the surface. When they sight prey, they dive down to chase it. In an experimental study common mergansers were far more likely to detect and dive toward a coho salmon parr if the fish was moving than if it was stationary (Martel and Dill 1995).

A complementary experiment showed that the water-borne odor of mergansers alone was sufficient to provoke predation-reducing behavior in coho (Martel and Dill 1993). Martel and Dill tested parr in an artificial stream for the distance they swam upstream to catch live brine shrimp as it drifted directly toward them in the current. In trials with no added odor or just fish odor, parr swam upstream about 11 cm to catch a shrimp, while in trials with merganser odor in the water, the young fish ventured only 8 cm upstream. Martel and Dill interpreted the difference in behavior to reflect an adaptive response by the fish to make themselves less likely to be moving and therefore less noticeable to an avian predator.

We have some evidence that trout do divide their attention between food and predators. Angradi (1992) tested wild juvenile trout collected from Henry's Fork of Idaho's Snake River for their reactions to simulated predator attacks in an artificial stream. The "attacks" involved plunging a dip net into the stream channel near a trout in an attempt to mimic the dive of an attacking belted kingfisher.

In a move that was important for elucidating the effect of divided attention on foraging, Angradi recorded the response of station-holding trout to each drifting brine shrimp, the food item he used. He categorized the response to each food item as either "consumption," where a fish swam out to and then ate a shrimp; "orient only," where a fish oriented toward but did not swim out to a shrimp; "reject," where a fish swam to, caught, and then spit out a shrimp; or "no response," where the fish maintained station and gave no evidence of having detected the passing shrimp. If we translate his terms to those used by signal detection theory, "consumption" might be considered a correct detection, "no response" a missed detection, "orient" a correct rejection, and "reject" a false alarm.

During a test one brine shrimp was drifted past a single station-holding fish every 30 seconds. After every fifth shrimp (2.5 minutes), experimental fish were accosted with the dip-net "predator," while controls were left undisturbed. Then he continued to monitor responses by fish in both treatment groups as they were presented with 25 more shrimp (12.5 minutes).

In the pre-predator period virtually all shrimp were taken by fish in both treatment and control groups, essentially a 100% rate of correct detections (figure 5.5). In the period just after an "attack," however, fish in the attacked group drastically reduced consumption (correct detections) from 100% to 55% of passing prey and increased the percentage of no response to shrimp (missed detection) to about 30.

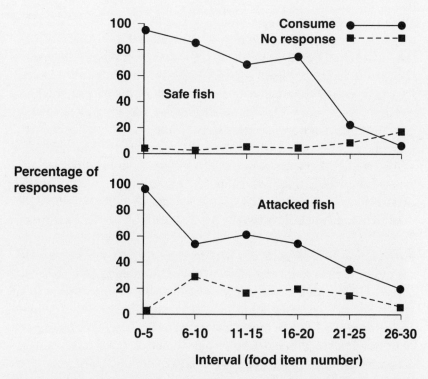

Figure 5.5. The Deadliness of Divided Attention. These graphs demonstrate the negative consequences of divided attention. Researchers used a dummy predator to "attack" juvenile rainbow trout that were holding station in an artificial stream as brine shrimp drifted by. The upper graph shows responses of control fish that were not "attacked." The lower graph shows feeding responses of fish before and after a simulated kingfisher attack between the fifth and sixth brine shrimp. As the researchers expected, attacked fish divided their attention between food and predator search; the trout drastically reduced their consumption rate (correct detections) and increased their no-response rate (missed detections) just after an attack. (Angradi 1992)

Meanwhile the consumption curve of the control trout gradually declined as the fish presumably became satiated, and the no-response rate (missed detection) remained low throughout.

In an experiment that complemented Angradi's project, Dill and Fraser (1984) tested the foraging responses of juvenile coho salmon to a simulated predator attack by using the reaction distance at which fish attacked prey instead of the proportion of prey consumed or not eliciting a response. In this case the "predator" was a photograph of a large rainbow trout that researchers moved forward and backward along the side of the artificial stream so that the juvenile salmon could see it. The reaction distance to prey was defined as the distance upstream to a surface-drifting fly when a station-holding fish first responded to it. Several sizes (species) of fly were used, but the response to the largest size seemed likely to be a result of divided attention between predator and prey. Fish not exposed to the trout photo first reacted when flies of this size were 30 cm upstream. After exposure to the trout photo, the young coho did not react until a fly had drifted to within about 20 cm upstream, a 33% reduction in reaction distance. Thus it is possible that by dividing their attention between detecting prey and looking out for their own predators, the juvenile salmon decreased the distinction between the signal (fly) and the background "noise."

Devoting some attention to competitors could also cause trout to compromise their ability to correctly detect food items. As I discussed earlier, Hughes's (1998) scenario for Alaskan grayling assumed that the fish sorted themselves out by social dominance along a food-temperature gradient. In such a system every fish except the largest and most powerful might be devoting some attention to monitoring its local surroundings for the attack of a bigger dominant fish, and such monitoring might provoke some missed detections of food. Records bearing on this possibility were collected from young-of-year Atlantic salmon holding station in an artificial stream under three different social conditions (Huntingford et al. 1993). Initially, the socially dominant member of each group of four fish was determined by observing which animal took up station farthest upstream toward the source of food pellets and, consequently, grasped the most food pellets. Then the stream's width was divided into three parallel compartments. One compartment housed the dominant parr and one subordinate. A second compartment held a second subordinate separated from the dominant by a transparent partition, so the dominant could see the subordinate but could not approach or chase it. The third compartment held the third subordinate behind an opaque partition that rendered it invisible to the dominant.

Several aspects of this study's results bear on what the effects of divided attention may be (figure 5.6). The subordinate housed with the dominant responded to only about 55% of the pellets coming down

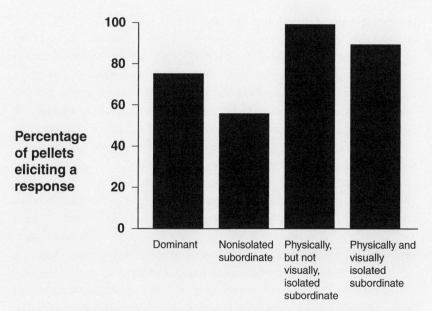

Figure 5.6. Social Dominance Status and Attention to Food. The percentage of food pellets eliciting a feeding response by Atlantic salmon parr under various social conditions demonstrates the effect of social dominance on attention to food. The two lefthand bars represent the feeding responses of a socially dominant and a socially subordinate fish living together in one channel of an artificial stream. The third bar and the one at far right display, respectively, the responses to food pellets of socially subordinate salmon separated from the dominant fish by a transparent and an opaque partition. Being either socially dominant or subordinate reduced a salmon's ability to detect food. (After Huntingford et al. 1993)

the channel, suggesting that it might have been dividing its attention between food and the dominant competitor. While the visually isolated subordinate responded to about 90% of the incoming pellets, the dominant housed with a subordinate responded to only about 75% of such food items. This difference suggests that the dominant may have been devoting some of its attention to the subordinate and therefore missed some detections. Finally, the subordinate protected by the transparent screen from aggressive attacks by the dominant displayed more correct detections than any other fish. This last result suggests that under such conditions of "benign competition" from dominants, a fish might actually devote more attention to food than would normally be the case.

In concluding this discussion of divided attention, I must return to the uncertainties of interpreting negative data. As I have suggested, the reduced consumption and increased "no responses" to prey by salmonids exposed to model predators or to attack by live dominant competitors could have been the result of divided attention. However, it is also possible that exposure to predators or dominant competitors had no effect at all on attention to prey. Instead, station-holding fish simply moved less as an adaptation to reduce the ability of predators to detect them or because they were intimidated by competitors from taking detected items. The crux of the issue is this: if a fish under predation risk or competitive pressure lets a prey item drift past, has it failed to detect the prey because of divided attention or has it in fact detected the prey and elected not to move to get it? Psychological methods such as those that I described for blue jays detecting cryptic moths should prove useful for answering this question about divided attention.

The next chapter considers more explicitly the ways in which an animal's own experience in its environment might also contribute to its foraging efficiency by increasing the distinction between signal and noise.

Chapter 6

Learning

Learning, any form of learning, has been defined as adaptive change in an individual's behavior as a result of experience (Thorpe 1963). In other words, an animal changes some aspect of its behavior because of something that has happened to it in its past, and because the change is adaptive, it must be in a direction that increases the animal's lifetime reproductive success. Following Thorpe (1963), I discuss several varieties of learning thought to be qualitatively distinct, before I turn to the mechanisms of memory, the storage of experiences required for learning to occur.

Habituation

The type of learning termed *habituation* involves stopping a response to an environmental stimulus if that stimulus is without significance to lifetime reproductive success (Thorpe 1963). As we will see, learning often results from positive or negative reinforcement of some particular behavior. In the realm of habituation psychologists believe that there are no reinforcements, either positive or negative. Thus they consider habituation to be learning what not to do in the absence of any reinforcement and have generally regarded it as the most primitive and widespread form of learning.

Many young animals are born with a tendency to react with alarm or avoidance to environmental stimuli that are large and rapidly moving, novel, appear suddenly, and/or are of high intensity. The adaptive function of habituation therefore seems to be as a filter that, after a number of encounters, lowers attention to stimuli without importance for fitness (lifetime reproductive success). A classical example is the land snail that displays the startle response of retracting its eye stalks less extensively each time it is stimulated mechanically; finally, it reaches complete habituation by refraining from withdrawing its eye stalks even when someone is bumping the ground next to it.

As any angler knows, trout show startle responses to nearby novel objects or movement. Several laboratory studies have shown that such responses can be eliminated with habituation. Wagner and Bosakowski (1994) provided indirect evidence of this phenomenon by setting a taxidermic mount of a bald eagle near hatchery-reared rainbow trout and gauging their reactions. Fish that had been reared under an overhead cover were tested in groups of four for their tendency to stay concealed under the cover in the presence of the stuffed eagle rather than swimming about in the two-thirds of the arena not covered. Over the course of 45 minutes, the average number of fish holding under cover waned from 3.8 to only 1.7 in 4, indicating habituation to the eagle's presence. (It would have been useful to learn how individual fish, tested alone, would have behaved, because then we could be confident that only the eagle and not their confreres influenced their behavior.

While the trout-eagle project focused on the results of behavior, namely, where the fish ended up every so often, a more direct demonstration of habituation at the behavioral level comes from a study of responses to extremely low frequency sound (Knudsen et al. 1997). The project was conceived to test the effectiveness of sound stimuli in preventing fish from entering irrigation canals or water inlets to hydroelectric power plants. A device containing a piston cycling at 60 Hz (60 cycles per second) was lowered into a tank containing a school of either young chinook salmon or young rainbow trout. Every time the school ventured within 1 m of the device, it was turned on for 5 seconds, and this procedure was repeated twenty times in succession. After an intervening 1-hour period, the researchers repeated the same series of stimuli. They tested eight schools of 15 to 25 individuals from each species. At each presentation of the sound the researchers coded the response of a school as either alarm, where the fish darted quickly away from the oscillating unit; avoidance, where the fish swam away from the sound at a brisk but not frenetic pace; or no response, where the fish acted as if they were ignoring the stimulus.

Both species demonstrated about the same degree of habituation to the sound stimulus (figure 6.1). All eight schools reacted with alarm at

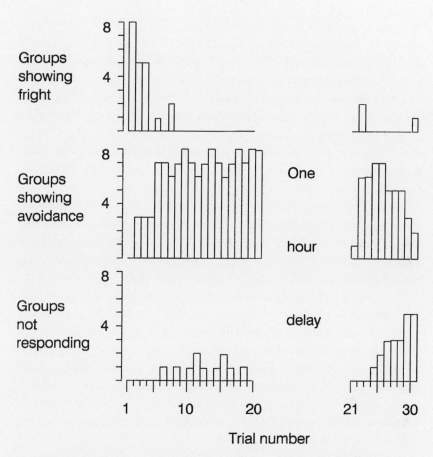

Figure 6.1. Habituation: The Simplest Form of Learning. Each time a group of captive juvenile rainbow trout approached within 1 m of a low-frequency (10 Hz, or 10 cycles per second) sound generator, the generator was turned on for 5 seconds. For the first 20 encounters with the sound source, the fish gradually changed from responding with fright (see top graph) to not responding at all (bottom graph), the defining feature of habituation. The fish showed that they remembered the experience because when they were retested after a 1-hour delay, they habituated more rapidly and more extensively than during the first series of trials, This can be seen by comparing trials 1 through 20 and 21 through 30 in the bottom graph of the figure. (After Knudsen et al. 1997)

first presentation and then switched increasingly to avoidance at intermediate points in the sequence of 20 sounds, with a few schools not responding in later presentations. These results indicate a strong short-term habituation in the alarm response, with the avoidance reaction considerably more resistant to habituation. Although I discuss memory in detail in the next chapter, it is interesting to note here the fish's response to the same sound stimulus after a 1-hour delay. It appeared that the fish had initially "forgotten" that they had habituated at all in the first session; seven of eight schools reacted with fright or avoidance. But note that in the second session the negative reaction dropped off more quickly, demonstrating some carryover from the earlier experience. Also, during the second session schools of fish had an increased tendency not to respond at all to the sound, demonstrating a more classical example of habituation where a behavioral pattern disappears altogether if it is not reinforced.

Before leaving the topic of habituation, I must report a thought-provoking anecdote. Not too long ago, my son, Josh, and I enjoyed a picnic lunch on a bank of the Firehole River in Yellowstone National Park. As we were lounging postprandially in the September sunshine, an osprey flew in to land high in a dead tree on the opposite side of the river. There it remained perfectly still except for moving its head as it scanned the water below. Perhaps 25 minutes later it suddenly plummeted into the stream, floated on the water with outstretched wings for perhaps a minute, then struggled into the air while clutching in its talons a rather hefty brown trout. Now suppose you are a trout-hunting osprey. How long do you think you should perch motionlessly on a branch before giving up and trying elsewhere? I doubt if anyone knows, but I will wager that the limit of the bird's patience is not unrelated to habituation time in trout.

Instrumental Learning

Psychologists believe that instrumental learning, also known as operant conditioning, is distinct from habituation. In instrumental learning an animal is conditioned through chance reinforcement to respond to a previously ignored stimulus (Thorpe 1963). Learning psychologists have defined *reinforcer* as any event that changes the probability that the behavior subsequent to reinforcement will recur in the future. Thus a reinforcer can be either positive, which would increase the probability of a response in the future, or negative, which would decrease the probability of the response. In the famous design of B. F. Skinner a caged animal such as a rat or a pigeon receives a food morsel soon after it performs some arbitrary behavior such as pressing a bar (rat) or pecking a colored spot (pigeon). When the animal has received rewards several times after a certain behavior, it comes to associate that particular behavior with the reinforcement, so the probability of the behavior increases. Conversely, if a behavior is followed by a negative reinforcer such as an electric shock, the probability of that behavior will lessen.

Clearly, instrumental learning is an extremely important influence in the lives of many animals, including trout. In a salmonid version of a Skinner box, rainbow trout received 10 to 12 food pellets each time they bumped or bit a metal trigger bar (Adron et al. 1973). Within groups of 30 fish the number of bar bumps in a 20-day period increased from about 1.6 per fish per day to about 9 per fish per day (figure 6.2), indicating that operant conditioning had been occurring. However, this is yet another result confounded by the design of the experiment, which did not explore whether the learning ability of some fish is affected by the presence of others, particularly social dominants. What might figure 6.2 look like for trout tested singly?

Operant conditioning would seem to be useful to a foraging trout in at least two major ways, separating signal from noise and increasing E/h ratios. In chapter 5 I discussed how the formation of specific search images might have the effect of separating in the mind of a trout the characteristics of a food signal from background sensory noise. Experiments that use operant conditioning with food as the positive reinforcement have shown that trout acquire such specific search images.

D. M. Ware (1971) demonstrated that wild-caught trout created a search image for a type of food that they had never encountered before. The novel food consisted of small cylindrical pieces of blanched chicken liver. On each of a number of consecutive days researchers scattered six liver nuggets on the black-painted floor of an aquarium into which they then introduced one fish. After 8 days of exposure to one trial per day, the trout reduced from 6 minutes to 30 seconds the time it needed to find all six baits. That is, the trout had learned by operant conditioning to recognize a new food type (figure 6.3). Furthermore, during the 8-day period the average distance from which trout reacted to a food item increased from 30 to 60 cm, evidence consistent with increasing ability to make correct detections (figure 6.3).

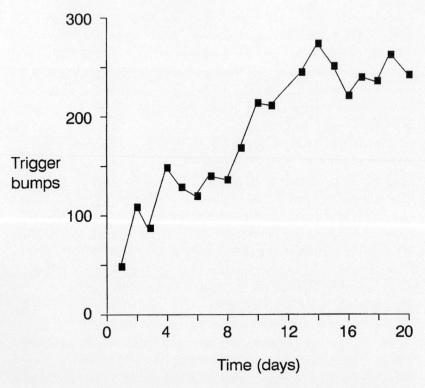

Figure 6.2. Rainbow Trout and Operant Conditioning. Groups of fish in a large aquarium were rewarded with food pellets for bumping a trigger bar. After 20 days of such positive reinforcement for the behavior, the trout displayed a sixfold increase in bar bumps per day. (After Adron et al. 1973)

Checking the trout's reaction to chicken bits that had been stained gray or black provided additional evidence of learning-induced specific search images. When trout conditioned to white pellets were confronted with black ones instead, their reactive distance immediately decreased from 60 to 20 cm, only to gradually increase during the next 9 days of exposure to six black-stained chicken bits (figure 6.4). Thus fish prepared by operant conditioning to form one specific search image appeared to require considerable experience before they could fully form another search image for a different-appearing food type. We can readily imagine similar mental processes occurring in trout in nature. I should point out a design problem in this study that weakens the in-

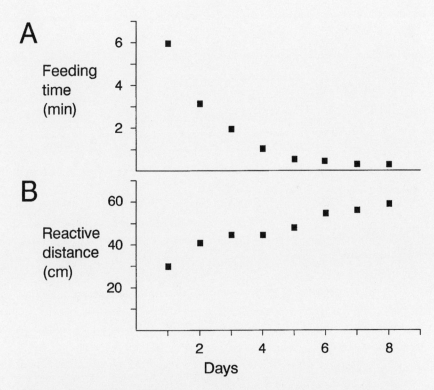

Figure 6.3. Operant Conditioning to a Food Source. In eight days trout learned to recognize as prey small cylindrical pieces of chicken liver that had been blanched white. As learning progressed, the time required to find six scattered pieces of food decreased (graph A), and the distance at which the fish first reacted to the food increased (graph B). (After Ware 1971)

terpretation of the results. Note that the original food type was white, the second food type was black, and the background was black. Could it be that the shorter reactive distance to the black food was due to its matching the background rather than to lack of a search image? An overarching effect of different contrasts between the two food signals and the background noise seems partially at work. Note that even after 9 days of experience, trout still did not react to black items as far away as they did white items. Nevertheless, the improved reaction to the black items over time buttresses the argument for a new search image. The results point out that in nature any reaction to a given food

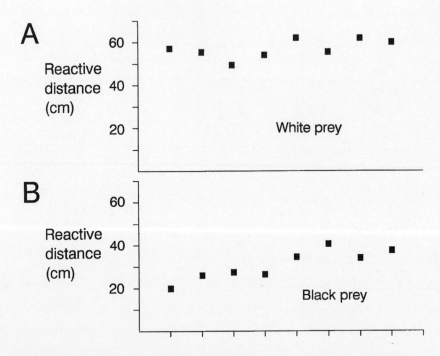

Figure 6.4. Operant Conditioning to Dyed Food Source. Trout conditioned to react at a distance to bits of white chicken liver (graph A) required considerable additional experience to recognize the same food after it had been stained black (graph B). (After Ware 1971)

type is likely to be a combination of both its initial signal contrast and the heightened perception resulting from a specific search image.

Irregularities in the spatial distribution of prey items could lead different trout to form different search images. In a large stream in August, for example, it might well be true that trout near shoreline vegetation have search images for hoppers and beetles, while those midstream do not. Trout have shown evidence of idiosyncratic search images even within the same spatial confines. In one study individual fish within quartets of rainbow trout allowed to forage within the same semiartificial pond displayed different diets (Bryan and Larkin 1972). In one group the stomach contents of one fish were 100% fly pupae, while another fish in the same pond had eaten only mayfly larvae. While the researchers chalked up such differences to variation in search images, it is important to remember that social dominance may have exerted a confounding effect, particularly because the researchers observed that different fish were catching food at different heights within the water column of the pond. Once again, testing individual fish in isolation would have been preferable.

Related to this issue of how a trout learns what to eat is the matter of how it learns what not to eat and how it avoids false alarms. Suppose that initially you caught oak leaves as well as every Frisbee. You might learn to concentrate on Frisbees because of positive reinforcement (say, the praise of others). But why would you stop catching leaves? This is an interesting question because it leads us to consider proximate and ultimate causation of behavior and how these two levels of causation can sometimes lead to conflicting interpretations.

Proximate causes of behavior are the current external (e.g., sound, temperature) and internal (e.g., hunger state) stimuli that cause an animal to behave in a certain fashion at any given instant. In contrast, ultimate causes of behavior are related to fitness and shape an animal's behavior in a way that increases lifetime reproductive success. Learning psychology has traditionally focused on proximate causation. According to such psychological thinking, habituation explains why you stopped catching oak leaves: your catching response was not followed by positive or negative reinforcement. Because nothing happened when you caught a leaf, you stopped. Similarly, it could be argued that because of a lack of either positive or negative reinforcement, a trout holding station in a stream habituates to any particular variety of debris drifting by.

Someone emphasizing ultimate causation of behavior would have a very different explanation for why a young trout eventually stops snapping at, say, drifting tulip-tree petals. In an ultimate sense the fish receives a negative reinforcement, namely, reduced net energy intake rate, for snapping at nonfood. So from the perspective of ultimate causation, operant conditioning, rather than habituation, is responsible for the loss of the response. In fact, from the perspective of ultimate causation, every response has some reinforcement, some consequences for fitness, so habituation does not exist.

We have no detailed evidence about how trout might learn not to respond to false alarms (debris in the drift). It seems possible that specific search images for nonfood could be involved. As part of their study of search images, Pietrewicz and Kamil (1981) tested the ability of blue jays to find camouflaged moths in photographic slides when pecking the slide was not reinforced. The birds learned to find the moths more quickly after seeing a run of slides of such moths.

The early theories of optimal diet selection assumed that foragers somehow had perfect knowledge of the ratio of energy to handling time for all types of food and that animals then used such E/h ratios to determine which food types to eat (figure 4.2). Because the perfect-knowledge assumption cannot be true, a current line of work focuses on how learning might aid animals in approximating E/h (Hughes 1979). Here I want to concentrate on how learning might decrease handling time and therefore increase the value of E/h of a particular food type by reducing the size of the denominator. Natural selection should favor any such ability.

Because the positive reinforcement involved is the food obtained, operant conditioning is the mechanism that reduces the time it takes a forager to manipulate a food item before ingesting it (Hughes et al. 1992). Of interest to us here is work that shows reduction in handling time with experience under conditions that ensure that a fish has already recognized an item as food. Croy and Hughes's work (1991) with the 15-spined stickleback, a small nonsalmonid fish living along ocean shores, meets this standard. Although Croy and Hughes examined the responses of these fish to several types of prey, I will focus only on the handling of a small amphipod, or scud, species, a common food in nature. During eight consecutive daily trials individual fish decreased their handling time per scud from about 17 seconds to about 6 seconds (figure 6.5). How did this reduction come about? The stickle-backs repeatedly spit out, recaptured, and then swallowed the first scuds that they took, and the spitting and capturing took time. Over several days the number of spit-outs per swallow decreased steadily, which meant the fish were becoming more efficient at handling prey (figure 6.6). Why were the fish spitting the scuds out less often? Scuds have rather hard prickly legs that point backward, so if a scud is attacked and captured head on, it can be swallowed immediately; otherwise, the predator must spit it out, reorient, and try again. Learning to attack head-on was the key to handling the scuds most efficiently, and

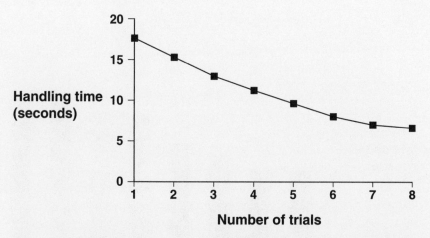

Figure 6.5. Operant Conditioning and the Efficient Handling of Food. Handling time is the number of seconds between the catching of a prey item and its being swallowed. Each point in the figure represents results from one of eight consecutive daily trials in which stickleback fish had to manipulate and swallow amphipod (scud) prey. Operant conditioning appeared to be responsible for the 50% reduction in handling time by the end of the period. (After Croy and Hughes 1991)

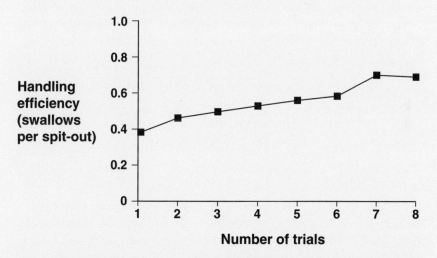

Figure 6.6. The Mechanism of Increased Handling Efficiency. A fish often would catch and then spit out a scud one or more times, apparently reorienting the prey item before swallowing it. The amount of time that it took a fish to eat a prey item was primarily determined by the spitting out and recapturing. Dividing each swallow by the number of preceding spit-outs provided a measure of handling efficiency. After eight days the sticklebacks almost doubled their efficiency by decreasing the number of times they spit out a prey item before finally swallowing it. Researchers attributed this change in behavior to operant conditioning. (After Croy and Hughes 1991)

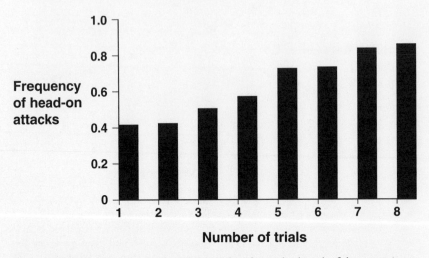

Figure 6.7. From Spit-Outs to Head-On Attack. After eight days the fish were twice as likely to attack a scud head-on. Because they always swallowed the scuds head first, the fish learned by operant conditioning that catching them head first decreased handling time and therefore increased the ratio of energy to handling time (E/h) for the prey items. Thus operant conditioning was responsible for the fish's acquiring food more rapidly. (After Croy and Hughes 1991)

it took the sticklebacks about seven or eight days to learn to do this (figure 6.7). Because the energy content of scuds remained constant, the sticklebacks used instrumental learning to increase the net energy value of this prey item by decreasing the denominator of the E/h ratio.

Classical Conditioning

Classical conditioning, a form of learning first described in the early twentieth century by the Russian physiologist Ivan Pavlov, shares with habituation the idea that animals have inborn, unlearned responses to certain external stimuli. Such bits of the environment are called *sign stimuli*. Their mere detection triggers a response. In the case of habituation an animal learns from experience to inhibit such responses when they have no consequences. For classical conditioning to occur, the animal must transfer the original unlearned response to a different, previously neutral stimulus. In the example developed so extensively by Pavlov, dogs would salivate in response to the presence of food, an unlearned response to the food sign stimulus. If a previously neutral stimulus such as a buzzer or bell were paired with the food for a number of trials, the dog would come to associate the sound with the food. Eventually, then, sound alone could induce salivation. Thus the animal had transferred an unlearned response to a new learned stimulus.

Salmonids have displayed classical conditioning under laboratory conditions, but the extent to which this form of learning is important in nature is less easy to envision than, say, habituation or operant conditioning. Commonly, classical conditioning has been a tool for probing the sensory abilities of trout and salmon. One project set out to determine how sensitive salmonids were to changes in water temperature (Bardach and Bjorklund 1957). Young rainbow trout exhibited an unlearned feeding response to food pellets, presumably based on one or more of the odor cues discussed in chapter 2. During each of 10 consecutive trials the researchers gradually cooled by 2°C the water in an aquarium containing young fish, then introduced a food pellet. By the end of the training session, the trout had exhibited classical conditioning; they had come to associate the lowering of water temperature with the food. As the aquarium water cooled, the trout would position themselves a short distance from the food-delivery tube, waiting for the food pellet. Actually, the fish responded well in advance of the full 2° drop, allowing the technique to demonstrate sensitivity to a temperature change of only 0.25°C.

One way that classical conditioning could be adaptive in nature might involve increasing the detection of signals associated with predators. An experiment addressing such a possibility capitalized on trout's having an unlearned fright or alarm response to chemicals released into the water from the skin of a trout damaged by a predator (Brown and Smith 1998). In this case the predator species was the northern pike, a serious menace to trout.

To produce a stimulus that would provoke an unlearned fright response, the researchers homogenized the skins of several freshly killed rainbow trout in a sample of distilled water that they then poured through a fiberglass filter to remove all particulate matter. The researchers produced the odor of pike, to which young rainbows were to be trained, by collecting a sample of water from an aquarium in which pike had been living for some time.

The question of interest was whether hatchery-reared trout would transfer by classical conditioning an unlearned fright response provoked by chemicals in damaged trout skin to a previously neutral stimulus, the odor of pike. In the first step of the study researchers observed groups of five fish for 10 minutes before introducing odors. In a nice design feature they exposed each group of fish to pike odor and distilled water in the morning and pike odor plus trout skin extract on the afternoon of the same day. Thus each group served as its own control.

This procedure clearly demonstrated that untrained trout ignored pike odor. Comparing behavior before and after they introduced odors, the researchers found that pike odor alone had essentially no effect on the tendency of trout to remain close to one another, a response termed *shoaling,* or to remain motionless. In contrast, when the pike odor was accompanied by trout skin extract, the young trout bunched into a tight shoal and tended to remain motionless (figure 6.8). After exposure to pike odor and trout skin extract combined, the young trout also took longer to capture their first brine shrimp, a food type provided during the tests, compared to their responses to pike odor alone. During a 10-minute period they ate fewer shrimp, fewer trout fed at all, and all animals remained in a smaller portion of the aquarium. Thus the first step of the project clearly demonstrated that young hatchery trout reacted strongly with alarm to chemicals produced by damaged trout skin but displayed no response to pike odor.

The next step in the study was to determine whether one exposure to the combination of pike odor and trout skin extract was sufficient for conditioning to occur, for trout to respond thereafter with fright to pike odor alone. Researchers reexamined three of the five fish in each group after a 4-day interval; they checked the other two fish after 21 days. As before, they compared fish behavior after presentation of a stimulus to behavior before presentation, only this time the researchers' interest focused on comparing responses after and before presentation of pike odor. In these latter tests the researchers examined the fish individually, so comparing shoaling responses was impossible.

Trout clearly transferred the alarm response to pike odor. Four days after one exposure to pike odor paired with trout skin extract, the young fish took longer to catch the first brine shrimp, ate fewer shrimp, spent more time under cover, and used a smaller portion of the aquar-

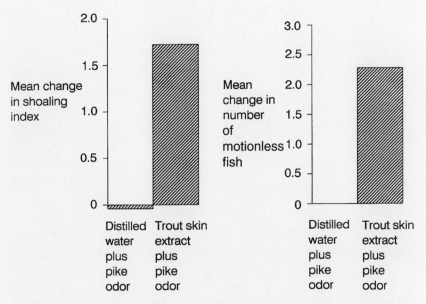

Figure 6.8. Classical Conditioning to Instill Antipredator Responses. Two behavioral indications of alarm to a predator in young rainbow trout are bunching together into a shoal and freezing into immobility. The odor of trout skin extract is known to elicit an unconditioned response in trout. That is, the fish would shoal and freeze on first encounter with the skin extract. As the figure shows, even though pike are serious predators of trout, the experimental trout had no unconditioned response to pike odor alone. The trout shoaled and froze when pike odor was introduced along with trout skin extract but not when pike odor was introduced alone. (After Brown and Smith 1998)

ium after being exposed to pike odor than to a similar volume of distilled water added to the aquarium. In addition, while no fish remained motionless after addition of only distilled water, almost half the animals adopted a motionless posture after detecting the added pike odor (figure 6.9). Twenty-one days after the initial one-time exposure, the trout still took longer to catch their first prey item and caught fewer brine shrimp after detecting the pike odor, but they no longer spent more time under cover, nor did they confine their movements to a smaller part of the aquarium. Notably, the proportion of fish adopting a motionless posture in response to pike odor was, if anything, higher after 21 days than after 4 days (figure 6.9).

Although its results are useful as an example of classical conditioning, this study was designed to demonstrate that reducing predation

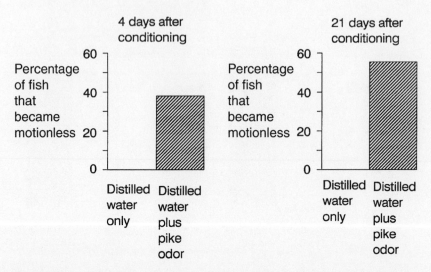

Figure 6.9. Learning to Fear Pike. Young trout were initially unresponsive to pike odor (see figure 6.8). However, 4 days and even 21 days after pike odor had been paired with trout skin extract, an odor that provokes an unlearned alarm response, the trout showed that they had retained the classically conditioned alarm response to pike odor alone. (Drawn from data in Brown and Smith 1998)

on newly released hatchery-reared trout was possible if, before release, the fish were trained to recognize characteristics of a predator. The learned cues were chemical in nature, so it would be worthwhile to see whether a similar training regimen would allow trout to respond to visual signals of predators. Could they learn to react with alarm to, say, the silhouette of a live heron, if a model heron were paired with trout skin extract? While transfer to visual cues has been shown in other fish (Chivers and Smith 1994), salmonids have not yet been tested (Brown and Smith 1998).

But the proof is in the pudding. Does such training in captivity actually increase the trout's rate of survival in nature after release? A recent study by another research group (Mirza and Chivers 2000) suggests that the answer to this question is maybe. Mirza and Chivers trained young brook trout to associate the alarm-producing odor of trout skin with the odor of a predator, this time a pickerel. The researchers knew from previous work that the skin of a tropical aquarium fish, the swordtail, did not provoke the alarm response in the trout.

They took advantage of this lack of response to create a control stimulus, namely, swordtail skin paired with pickerel odor. The result of the training was two groups of trout, one trained to react with alarm to pickerel odor, the other not. What happens when these groups are actually exposed to a pickerel? Would the knowledge of the trained fish allow them to survive better in the presence of the predator? At first blush the answer was yes. Researchers left 10 trained trout and 10 untrained trout for 4 hours in the company of one pickerel in each of seven midstream cages. Who survived? On average, 9.7 trained trout survived and 9.1 untrained trout. This result was statistically significant, so the authors were justified in concluding that learning to recognize a predator had a real effect on survivorship. The result is even more impressive when we note that the researchers had identified the trout in the two groups by snipping off a bit of the upper tail fin in one group and the lower tail fin in the other. Thus the untrained trout could have detected the alarm-inducing sign stimulus from the cut fins. That is, if the fish in the control group reacted with alarm to the odor of their own cut fins, that reaction would have made their behavior more similar to that of fish in the experimental group, biasing results against finding a difference in response between the two groups.

Earlier I said that the answer to the survivorship question was maybe, and the reason it is maybe is that fitness is relative. Let me illustrate this idea with a little story. Two intrepid youngsters are preparing for a backpacking fishing trip into the interior of Alaska. Before they jump off from Fairbanks, one buys a new pair of running shoes. When her partner asks why, she says so she can run fast in case they are attacked by a grizzly bear. Her partner scoffs at the idea; even new shoes will not enable her to outrun a bear.

"I don't have to outrun the bear," she replies, "I just have to outrun you!"

In the present case we know that when 10 trained trout and 10 untrained trout were exposed together to a pickerel predator for 4 hours, the trained fish survived better. But suppose all 20 trout were trained— would they survive better than 20 untrained trout? Probably not, according to results of another experiment reported in the same article. In that experiment, conducted in a laboratory aquarium, it took a pickerel just as long to capture one of three untrained trout as it did to capture one of three trained trout. If we are to know that training stocked fish aids their survival, someone needs to show that over the course of days or weeks, a population consisting entirely of trained fish survives better (i.e., has greater relative fitness) than a similar-sized population of untrained fish.

Latent Learning

According to Thorpe (1963), latent learning is the association of indifferent stimuli, or situations without obvious reward. Thus latent learning differs in important ways from the other kinds of learning that I have discussed because it occurs, so far as we can tell, in the absence of any immediate fitness benefits. The key to understanding how natural selection might have favored latent learning is to realize that the benefits of learning can be deferred. No one has made experimental demonstrations of latent learning in trout, so a brief description of a classic example from psychology is in order (Tolman and Honzik 1930). Tolman and Honzik allowed two groups of rats to negotiate a maze, one at a time. They rewarded rats in one group with food at a particular location. Not surprisingly, the rats learned by operant conditioning to find that spot in the maze. After 10 days of such learning trials, they could scurry right to the food. When rats of the previously unrewarded group were rewarded with food for the first time on day 11, they quickly improved their performance to match that of the continually rewarded group. The conclusion from this experiment was that even when not obtaining any noticeable reward, rats were learning the layout of the maze. Why? An argument can be made that potentially useful information can enhance the fitness of animals with good memories. Such learning remains latent, unknown to an outside observer, until the animal finds some adaptive use for it.

Although experimental demonstrations are lacking for salmonids, descriptive evidence suggests that they may be capable of latent learning. In Wyoming (Young 1996) and Colorado (Gowan et al. 1994) telemetry studies revealed that trout often moved hundreds of meters in short periods for no apparent reason. Perhaps the trout moved to learn about the stream habitat. Rainbow trout were much more likely than brown trout to move extensively in a small stream in southern

Idaho (Young et al. 1997). Could rainbows have more of a tendency to engage in latent learning? If so, why?

And what might it be useful to learn latently? In streams that are subject to summer warming, knowledge obtained in the spring about the location of cool, spring-fed pools could confer a fitness advantage later in the year. Young steelhead found their way to cool water at the base of deep, thermally stratified pools, thus avoiding summer water temperatures as high as 28°C in other reaches of a river (Nielsen et al. 1994). Many anglers have had the experience of a newly hooked trout that immediately swims up- or downstream some considerable distance to protective cover. One can imagine the value of latently learning the locations of such refuges. Presumably, trout remember such latently learned sites in conjunction with cognitive maps, a matter I discuss later.

Imprinting

Konrad Lorenz, the Austrian student of animal behavior, first brought the phenomenon of imprinting to prominence (Hess 1973). Within a few hours of being born, certain birds such as chickens and ducks, and mammals such as antelope and deer, can walk or run. Such ability is thought to be adaptive in reducing the risk of being killed by predators at the birth site. Lorenz found that the young animals learned the characteristics of the parents that they then followed, and he called this form of learning *imprinting* because it had some peculiar properties that set it apart from other forms. Imprinting of an object to be followed occurred during a brief period early in an animal's life but not in later periods. Other forms of learning, such as those that I have been discussing, were thought to operate throughout a lifetime. Researchers showed that young chicks could be most successfully imprinted about 16 hours after they hatched and even with such disparate objects as red watering cans and spinning lights.

In these imprintable birds and mammals Lorenz found that the imprinted memory was long lasting and was later influential in determining the object of sexual activity. At maturity such animals would often court and attempt to mate with the same type of object on which they had been imprinted at an early age. Such behavior was thought to be adaptive because under normal conditions an imprinted animal would attempt to mate with a member of its own species.

Not long after Lorenz described social imprinting, researchers found that animals could also make early and lasting attachments to particular habitat features, and they found that one of the more powerful examples of habitat imprinting occurred in certain salmonids. Between their birth and their departure for the ocean or large lake, young migratory salmonids imprint on their natal stream, and they do this by memorizing that stream's particular mixture of odors.

Hara (1993) has proposed two major mechanisms to explain such olfactory habitat imprinting. The olfactory hypothesis, the better known of the two, holds that while they are transforming from parr to smolts shortly before heading downstream, young salmon memorize, in just days or even hours, the olfactory "landscape" of the home stream. The imprinting is thought to be caused by a surge in thyroxine, which stimulates neural development in the olfactory system (Dittman and Quinn 1996).

The olfactory hypothesis has two notable features. First, olfactory imprinting is believed to occur only during one relatively short period in a fish's life. Second, fish can remember for years and over thousands of kilometers the precise cocktail of odors unique to their home stream. The theory holds that once other forms of navigation at sea have gotten salmonids to the vicinity of their home stream, their remarkable olfactory memory takes over to guide the series of left-right decisions on their way upstream to their home site.

Strong experimental evidence supports the olfactory hypothesis for habitat imprinting. If salmon parr are moved from their birth stream to another before they become smolts and are then allowed to proceed with their lives, they will go to sea and later return to the stream to which they were displaced, not the stream of their birth. Furthermore, an elegant series of experiments showed that salmon would even return to breed at a site where they had been exposed to an artificial odor as young fish so long as that artificial odor was still present at the site (Hasler and Scholz 1983).

The second hypothesis about imprinting, termed the *pheromone hypothesis*, is really a subsidiary of the olfactory hypothesis. The pheromone hypothesis holds that the population of juvenile salmon inhabiting any particular stream has, in the aggregate, an odor fingerprint. Before smolting, young salmon imprint on this fingerprint. The argument goes that because the same population continues to inhabit the focal stream over the years, all a returning fish has to do to get home is follow the memorized odor trail to its relatives. The mucus from fish in each population is thought to provide the distinctive cue, and although one study reported that Arctic char responded differently to water from home and foreign populations of the same species (Døving et al. 1975), a similar study with brook trout was not able to show that brook trout responded differentially to water from home and foreign populations of the same species (Keefe and Winn 1991). Regardless of the results of such discrimination tests, the pheromone hypothesis clearly is not sufficient to explain the homing behavior of young salmon displaced from their home stream and relatives by Hasler and his colleagues. It seems more likely that the odors emanating from juvenile conspecifics are just part of the complex imprinting cocktail that has been so well documented.

While the prevailing general theory holds that imprinting is confined to just one brief period in a young animal's life, the so-called critical or sensitive period, further consideration suggests that salmonids with complex life cycles may have more than one critical period. For example, in the winter some coho salmon move downstream, before smolting, from the small tributaries where they were born. They later change from parr to smolt in the larger rivers downstream, so if the only critical period for imprinting occurred just before smolting, such fish should have no strong memory of the odor of the natal stream. Yet such fish do return to the natal stream. This and similar observations have prompted the notion that salmonids can and often do imprint at several times and places before and during their downstream journey (Dittman and Quinn 1996). However, the mechanisms for such multiple imprinting have not been worked out fully because young fish, at least those reared in hatcheries, were not sensitive to imprinting odors before the smolting period (Dittman et al. 1996).

Why should salmonids have evolved such remarkable habitat imprinting? The answer seems to be to make sure that they return to their birth site. All right, you ask, then why is such a precise return a good thing? That question is at the heart of a big subject, which is known as the evolution of life history strategies. Any substantial discussion of life history theory is beyond the scope of this book, but briefly, there are two main ideas about why returning to breed at the birth site increases lifetime reproductive success, and these ideas may not be mutually exclusive. First, animals are thought to return with precision so they can breed with relatives. Breeding with relatives promotes the formation of what are called *co-adapted gene complexes*. Because the genetic structure of two breeding relatives is not likely to be very different, the expression of the effects of maternal and paternal genes would not be in conflict (Shields 1982). The second idea has been termed the *ecogenetic hypothesis* (Shields 1982). According to this idea, animal populations could become genetically adapted to certain unique characteristics of a local environment. By returning to breed in precisely the same place where they were born, salmonids would capitalize on any local adaptations they might have inherited. For example, populations of sockeye salmon breeding in various streams of the Kvichak River system in Alaska vary in the size of both breeding males and eggs (Blair et al. 1993). It turns out that salmon that are breeding in streams with smaller gravel lay smaller eggs. Also, males breeding in shallower rivers are smaller and have a less noticeable hump. Some researchers have argued that in such shallower streams the increased predation on large hump-backed males by bears overrides the usual preference of female salmon to breed with large hump-backed males. (Note how this argument invokes the diet selection of the bear as a factor in the evolution of salmon body shape.) The main point here is that such genetic adaptation to local variation in the environment can only be accomplished if animals bearing genes for such adaptations breed with other such animals. A precise homing mechanism guided by stream-specific odors learned by imprinting allows such animals to find each other for breeding.

Social Learning

Imitating the behavior of others is called *social learning*. Such imitation can involve copying the actions of another animal at a certain place (*local enhancement*) or independent of a specific site (*social facilitation*) (Thorpe 1963).

Valone (1996) has suggested that an animal looking for food uses both "private information" about the results of its own food seeking and "public information" obtained by observing the feeding success of animals around it. A famous and well-documented example of public information occurred soon after World War II when, presumably, a single individual animal of a British songbird species learned to peck through the foil covers of milk bottles and drink the cream from the top of the milk. The first bird to perform this annoying feat almost certainly acquired the habit by instrumental learning. More interesting for a discussion of social learning, the habit spread quickly to birds in a large area of southern England, forcing homemakers to begin using covered milk boxes. The birds apparently were keeping close watch on the food-finding activities of their neighbors.

We have no records of trout that have copied the novel activities of other fish, but a fish's behavior can be influenced by the presence of neighbors. Within an experimental apparatus young brown trout in a group took food items more quickly and ate more than when they were in social isolation. However, Sundström and Johnsson (2001) correctly pointed out that such behavior could have been less the result of social learning and more because of perceived competition for food or a perceived reduction in predation risk in the company of another fish.

While experimental evidence for true social learning is not available for salmonids, Laland and colleagues have been pursuing the matter with guppies. In one study Laland and Williams (1997) trained an adult female guppy to take one of two routes to the same food source. Then, for 5 days an untrained female was allowed to follow the so-called demonstrator to the food. The critical question was which of the two routes the follower would take after the demonstrator had been removed. In a nicely balanced experiment the newly isolated followers used the route that they had learned from the demonstrator. Furthermore, by gradually replacing experienced with untrained fish, the researchers showed a kind of cultural transmission of the behavior, so that eventually guppy schools chose one route or the other as a matter of tradition even though none of the fish had learned the route by direct personal observation.

Chapter 7

Memory

Without a mechanism for storing the results of experience, namely, memory, an animal cannot learn. In this chapter I will briefly review some current thinking about the general attributes of memory (Manning and Dawkins 1998), then turn to what we know about memory storage in trout and their relatives.

Most of our current thinking about the mechanisms and anatomical locations of memory come from work with rats, young chickens, and honey bees (Manning and Dawkins 1998), so applying such conclusions to trout requires caution. Nevertheless, the notion that the brain has both temporary and more permanent sites of memory storage is likely to hold for salmonids. The general findings are that memories are stored initially within circuits of actively firing cells and later transformed into permanent storage during production of new (protein-containing) cells. Baby chicks trained to associate a certain color of glass bead with a bad taste would thereafter refuse to pick up beads of that color. However, the use of specific drugs revealed that the birds temporarily lost the avoidance response twice, the first about 15 minutes after learning it and again about 40 minutes after that (Andrew 1985). Such evidence led to the conclusion that memory storage occurs in three phases and that the two periods of memory lapse marked brief intervals when the system was "down" during data transfer from one form of memory to another. The first two stages proved to be temporary and the third permanent. Drugs that block transfer to the third stage lead to memory loss, but memories that reach the third stage are at least semipermanent. Interestingly, while rats show the same sort of three-phase memory process, honeybees require only two phases (Menzel et al. 1993).

Before turning to the existing evidence for memory ability in trout, I should mention a gap in our general conceptual understanding that could be filled nicely by work with salmonids. We know essentially nothing about the effect of body temperature on learning and memory, yet we might imagine from first principles of physiology (the "Q_{10} rule" [Davson 1964]) that processes involved with memory should double in rate with each 10°C rise in temperature, as do all known physiological processes. It is quite clear that trout must be able to learn and remember with body temperatures that vary with time, day, and season. How does temperature affect the rate at which the fish learn? Do trout store long-term memory of a new food source four times faster at 25°C than at 5°C? Does water temperature have any influence on the length of memory retention? What happens to learning and memory if the water (and trout) temperature varies greatly among learning episodes? What are the implications for lifetime reproductive success if trout can learn much faster in warmer water than in colder? If they can remember better in warmer water, can they remember more types of food then and therefore widen their optimal diet?

While I am at it, what is the effect of water temperature on perception and attention? Certainly, trout on the line behave sluggishly in water of, say, 4°C. Are they correspondingly less perceptive and attentive then?

For how long can trout remember things? This question has been addressed in passing by researchers more interested in how fast the fish learned in the first place. Ringler (1985) showed that brown trout could retain for at least 24 days a memory for avoiding an unpalatable prey type (woolly bear caterpillars). Rainbow trout taught to take novel and distinctively colored food items remembered the task for at least 2 weeks but had completely forgotten after 3 months; by that time they had to be taught all over again (Ware 1971) (see figure 7.1). However, a study of rainbow trout taught to press a bar for a food reward refuted the idea that trout have a maximum memory window of less than 90 days. Even after being hand-fed for 3 months, the fish immediately went back to on-demand feeding when again given the opportunity to bar press (Adron et al. 1973).

Studies with sticklebacks augment our knowledge of memory retention in trout. Remember that optimal diet selection theory holds

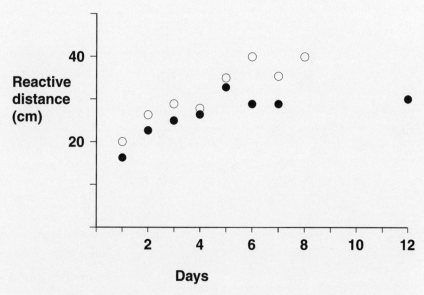

Figure 7.1. Memory in Young Rainbow Trout. As one- and two-year-old trout learned that small pieces of black-dyed liver were food, the fish reacted to the food from a greater distance away. In 10 days their reaction distance increased from about 20 to 40 cm, an indication that learning had occurred (open circles). However, when retested after a hiatus of 90 days, the fish showed that they had completely forgotten about the food type (closed circles). Their reaction distance began at the same low level as initially and did not improve any faster. (After Ware 1971)

that the handling time per prey item is an important variable, the shorter the better. One study set out to determine whether sticklebacks could decrease their handling time of various prey types with experience (Croy and Hughes 1991). Sticklebacks first presented with scuds as prey took considerable time in catching and orienting them for swallowing (figure 7.2). The legs of the little crustacean point backward along the body, and the sticklebacks learned from experience to quickly orient the scud head-first so it would get down more easily. Of interest to this discussion was the length of the memory for the new handling technique. The fish completely forgot after only 8 days, doing no better after that time interval than naive (untrained) fish.

Another stickleback study examined the maximum memory length for particular food patches (Milinski 1994). Fish in an aquarium were trained to expect food in one of two patches and then tested for their

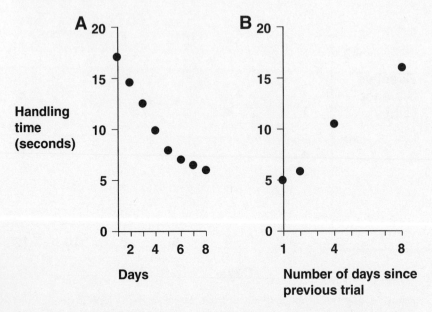

Figure 7.2. Stickleback Memory Loss. Sticklebacks took about eight attempts to learn how to eat scuds efficiently by swallowing the little crustaceans head first (graph A). The fish gradually forgot the efficient handling technique that they had learned until, after a lapse of 8 days, they were no more efficient than when completely naive (graph B). (Croy and Hughes 1991)

preference 1 to 14 days later. Although the test fish exhibited considerable differences, on average they seemed to retain some memory for the food-rich patch for about 8 days.

The results of these memory experiments foster the impression that while ordinary memory traces are labile, they last no longer than several months. In contrast, recall the phenomenon of salmonid olfactory imprinting to the home stream, a process involving a memory lasting on the order of years. In terms of ultimate or evolutionary causation, one obvious explanation for the difference in memory length concerns the value of forgetting. While a trout may relearn on a day-to-day basis the food items that are most valuable (because of E/h considerations, for example), it need learn only once the distinctive odor of its home stream. It must not forget that odor, and it need not learn the odor of any other stream.

In concluding this chapter I return again to the role that temperature may play, this time in memory retention. As we would expect from good experiments, the studies that I have cited here took pains to control the temperature of a trout's surroundings. For this reason they can provide no help in determining whether a fish living in cold water is likely to retain memory traces longer than one in warmer water, or the reverse. I hope that someone soon will perform the relevant experiment. If memory span does turn out to be temperature dependent, it may help to explain some of the temperature preferences of trout during the year.

Chapter 8

Cognitive Maps

Consider your own cognitive map. You know where you are now on the surface of the earth. You know where the food store is and also where the movie theater is. One school of thought holds that in order to demonstrate your ability to form a cognitive map, you must be able to get from the food store to the movie theater on your first try. That is, your mental map must be able to tell you the spatial relationship between the store and theater without your ever having seen the relationship directly (Tolman 1948). Other researchers ascribe to the less stringent idea that a cognitive map can be any spatial representation that aids in efficient foraging or quick escapes to cover (Braithwaite et al. 1996).

In the section on latent learning in chapter 6, I mentioned that telemetry studies clearly show that trout routinely move great distances on a daily basis. During such trips they might have ample opportunities to build up a mental depiction of their home waters. In a Norwegian project (Halvorsen and Stabell 1990) brown trout were taken from their home tributary stream and released in the parent river 150 meters upstream from the entry point of their home tributary. Within nine weeks 24% of the fish were found back at the capture site. This result is consistent, at least, with the idea of a spatial sense. A companion experiment compared the homing ability of control fish with those deprived of a sense of smell. While 40% of the controls returned to the capture site, few in the treatment group did so. Thus trout may form maplike representations that have a strong basis in their olfactory perceptions of the neighborhood, which is not too surprising given the ability of salmon on spawning runs to locate the natal site by its odor.

Limited experimental evidence exists for cognitive maps in fish. I will review two studies with goldfish, a lab rat of the fish world, before examining work in Scotland on spatial learning in juvenile Atlantic salmon. Warburton (1990) demonstrated that goldfish can learn the relationship between landmarks and the location of a hidden food source. He sank two ice-cube trays flush with the gravel bottom of a fish tank such that they occupied mirror-image positions in an aquarium. He filled all 12 compartments in each tray with sand. But in one tray he buried a flake of fish food under the sand in 4 of the 6 compartments closer to the midline of the aquarium. All 12 compartments of the other tray were left foodless. Random selection guided the choice of tray in which to place the food. The experiment also used several kinds of landmarks; here I will focus on one, a tower of Lego blocks. In the treatment group Warburton positioned this tower next to the tray with the food, while the control aquarium lacked any sort of landmark.

The fish showed that they could learn the spatial relationship between food location and a conspicuous visual landmark (figure 8.1). During 12 learning trials the fish chose the food tray with increasing probability until by the last trial all eight fish foraged in the food tray first. Control fish split their foraging priority between the two trays. When Warburton switched the food to the tray away from the Lego tower, the fish initially made the expected mistake of going to the Lego tray first. By the thirteenth trial in the food-switched scenario, about two-thirds of the fish had mentally reversed the spatial relationship and were now going first to the nontower tray. This experiment showed quite clearly that goldfish, at least, form mental images of the spatial relationships between parts of their environment and take a while to bring such mental patterns into agreement with a changed environment.

A second experiment asked a more sophisticated question: How do goldfish use their cognitive maps to determine how far they are from a fixture in the environment? R. H. Douglas (1990) examined two possibilities. The first was that the size of an object tells the goldfish how far away it is. For example, if you know the size of the water tower in your town, you can use its apparent size (that is, its angular size on your retina) as a clue to how far away it is. Alternatively, for objects that are not constant in actual size, you would need to use a combined judgment of any given object's size and some other measure of distance to tell how far away it is. In Douglas's experiment the methodology con-

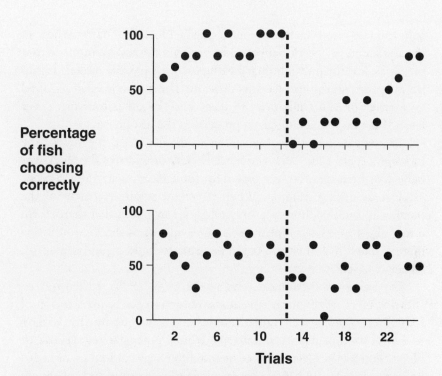

Figure 8.1. Evidence for a Cognitive Map in Goldfish. The upper graph shows that by the twelfth day of finding food buried beneath sand in an ice cube tray next to a Lego-block tower, 100% of 10 fish tested looked for food there before trying another ice cube tray away from the Legos. After day 12, when the food was switched to the tray away from the Legos, the fish initially continued to try the Lego tray first, but after 9 or 10 more trials, the majority of fish had switched to checking the non-Lego tray first. The lower graph shows that control fish with no Lego landmarks tried each tray about half the time, as would be expected if they had no preference throughout the experiment. (After Warburton 1990)

sisted of training goldfish to seek hidden food at one particular distance from a landmark, then changing the size of the landmark. If the goldfish used apparent landmark size alone to judge distance, they should have foraged closer to the landmark when it was made smaller because it would then appear to them to be farther away from the food. Conversely, if the landmark size were made larger than during training trials, the fish should seek food farther away because it would appear closer than the training stimulus.

In an otherwise featureless aquarium Douglas trained goldfish to seek food 20 cm in front of a black plastic block, no matter where in the aquarium the block happened to be. This method guaranteed that the block was the only landmark being used. Of passing interest is that training the fish to this task was difficult. Three of seven fish required an average of 175 trials over 35 days, and the other four fish never learned the task well enough to proceed to the test phase.

At any rate, the three fish showed that they used the size of the block as a spatial cue. When either the height or width of the block was halved, as predicted the fish looked for food 10 cm away from it, twice as close as during training. When either the width or height of the block was doubled, however, only one fish foraged farther than 20 cm away. This project thus furnishes some evidence of the kind of information that a fish in nature could be using to build cognitive maps of its environment.

The salmon experiment (Braithwaite et al. 1996) started out by showing nicely that young fish can use color as a cue to the location of food. Braithwaite's team trained youngsters in an aquarium for 14 days to expect food pellets to be delivered from a pipe near red, yellow, or blue Lego blocks. A second pipe near a differently colored set of Legos never produced food pellets. Between trials Braithwaite and colleagues randomly varied the positions of the food-producing pipe and the color of the blocks associated with it, to guarantee that the fish were using the colored blocks and not something else in the aquarium as the position cue. The test came during the next 10 days when the researchers noted the Lego color where the fish held just before being fed. If the fish used the color cue, the prediction was that they would stay near the color that had been paired with the food-delivering pipe, regardless of the position of that pipe. Once again, a fair number of fish did not associate color and food during the learning trials, instead favoring one side or the other of the aquarium, regardless of the position of the food source. Of the six fish that did not have a position preference, all followed reasonably well the Lego color associated with food during the 10-day test period (figure 8.2).

A problem developed during the second phase of the experiment. The researchers presented each color-following fish with the food-associated Lego color in front of both pipes. If the fish then became confused about which pipe would deliver the food, that result would

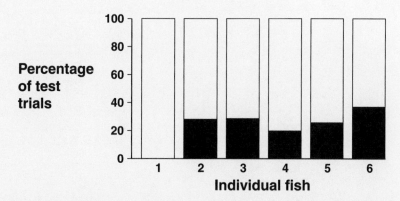

Figure 8.2. Evidence for a Cognitive Map in Atlantic Salmon Parr. For 14 days researchers trained young salmon to expect food delivery from a pipe located near only one of two differently colored Lego squares on the floor of the aquarium. The position of the Lego squares was randomly determined for each day's training. During each day of the 10-day test phase that followed, the researchers noted which square the fish held near while waiting for the food to be delivered. By mostly waiting near the training color (open part of each bar), all six fish tested showed they had associated the presence of food with a local landmark. (After Braithwaite et al. 1996)

help to confirm that color was serving as a spatial cue. But the fish did not cooperate and instead continued to be found on the food-pipe side of the aquarium, even when both sides had the same Lego color. The authors were forced to suggest that the fish must have been using some other cue, and they settled on olfaction as most likely. At any rate, this seems to be the only experimental demonstration of a salmonid's forming a spatial representation of its surroundings based on external cues.

Chapter 9

State-Dependent Cognition

Quite good evidence exists that much, if not all, trout thinking is in fact state dependent. Examples include the influence of two internal factors, social dominance status and hunger state.

Dominance

In practice we measure the social dominance relationship between any two animals by noting such things as who chases or bites whom, who has first access to any particular resource in short supply (such as an energy-efficient feeding station in a stream), and who avoids another animal by moving away at its approach. Within any given trout species dominance status is a function of size; larger fish dominate smaller ones (Abbott et al. 1985). This brings up the point that the state of any animal's dominance is depends on the context. The same fish can quickly shift dominance status if the size distribution of the fish around it changes.

The effects of dominance can be studied among members of the same or different species. Researchers have devoted a good deal of attention to cross-species dominance in trout to see whether this might explain why an introduced species sometimes appears to displace another from its native range. As one example of many, in a lab study young brown trout dominated young cutthroat trout, displacing the latter from good foraging locations (Wang and White 1994). This cross-species result violated the usual within-species size-dominance rule because the brown trout dominated cutthroats that were as much as 1.7 times heavier.

Several categories of Atlantic salmon parr feeding in an artificial stream shed considerable light on how dominance status can affect feeding rate and therefore growth rate (Huntingford et al. 1993). I have already mentioned this well thought-out study in relation to the matter of attention, so I will only briefly reiterate the methods here. After the researchers had identified the dominant fish in a group of four, they introduced each of the four young salmon into one of three parallel chambers aligned with current flow. The arrangement was such that the dominant and one subordinate fish shared one chamber. A second subordinate was placed next door in a chamber separated from that of the dominant by a clear piece of glass, so the dominant could see it but not chase it. The third subordinate was placed on the other side of the dominant in a chamber separated by an opaque partition. Thus the dominant could not see this fish.

Subordinate status clearly interfered with feeding; the subordinate fully exposed to the dominant reacted to fewer food pellets floating by than did the dominant (figure 5.6). However, both subordinates physically separated from the dominant fed actively, so visual exposure alone was not enough to suppress feeding. Interestingly, both the dominant and the visually exposed subordinate reacted to the presence of a potential competitor by attacking food items farther away than did the visually isolated subordinate parr. Thus the visually separated fish was apparently more able to follow optimal foraging rules by allowing far distant (higher handling time) items to pass by. Faced with apparent competition for food, the dominant and the visually exposed subordinate overrode the optimality rule. The final item of note in this study was that in a social system even dominant fish can be negatively influenced by the dominance relationship. Perhaps the dominant fish's having to divide its attention between food and the location of the subordinate caused the dominant fish to eat only a little more than 60% of passing food pellets, while both subordinates housed in the adjoining chambers did better (figure 9.1).

In the salmon example all the fish were familiar with each other, shown by their formation of stable dominance relationships. Maybe there is some advantage, in terms of lifetime reproductive success, to living in a dominance relationship with other known individuals, whether a fish is dominant or subordinate, rather than having to exist in the company of strangers. Imagine, for example, enormous schools

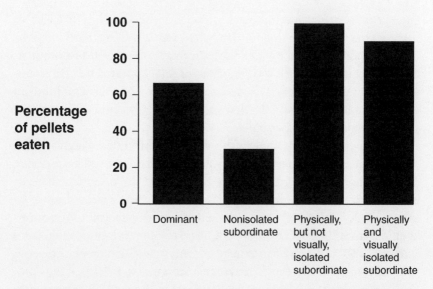

Figure 9.1. Effect of Social Dominance on Food Consumption in Atlantic Salmon Parr. A socially dominant fish housed with a subordinate consumed fewer food pellets than did either a subordinate physically separated from the dominant or a subordinate both physically and visually separated from the dominant. As might be expected, a socially subordinate fish in the immediate vicinity of a dominant ate few drifting food pellets. More interesting, a comparison of the lefthand bars in this figure and in figure 5.6 reveals that the dominant did not consume every food pellet to which it responded. Perhaps the attention it paid to its roommate was responsible for this reduction in food consumption by a dominant fish compared to that of the isolated subordinates. (After Huntingford et al. 1993)

of salmon at sea where the individuals might have little chance to create and maintain a stable dominance hierarchy. However, for salmonids living in small groups, like the ham-eating brook trout in the Grand Tetons that I mentioned earlier, conditions could permit formation of stable dominance-ordered groups. Johnsson (1997) used rainbow trout to look for advantages to living in such groups.

Johnsson placed young rainbow trout of similar size in pairs within aquaria. For 3 days he fed each pair a less-than-adequate number of trout pellets, and he assumed that the fish that ate more of them was socially dominant. He also noted the number of attacks that each fish made on the other. Then he assigned the pairs to various groups, some of which are pertinent here. The next day Johnsson retested pairs in one group for their level of aggression toward each other. In order to see the effect of a known dominance relationship on aggression levels, Johnsson also retested the next day the aggression levels of dominant and subordinate fish in a second group of unacquainted fish. To examine the stability of social arrangements, in a third group, Johnson treated the fish as he had the first group but 3 days later separated the two fish physically and visually.

A stable dominance relationship decreased the rate of aggression in a way that was beneficial to both dominant and subordinate (figure 9.2). Compared to retesting with each other, the dominant fish attacked strange fish more and the subordinate was attacked more by strange fish. Thus for both fish the reduction in aggressive interactions would permit them to pay more attention to other important functions such as food and predator detection. The social advantage, however, was fleeting. When retested 3 days later the aggression level of the dominant rose slightly above that of first testing (figure 9.2). Apparently, 3 days of separation were sufficient for a fish to forget who the other was. In nature, however, it is unlikely that a fish will become separated from its group, so the advantages of social hierarchies should hold. A moral in this story for catch-and-release anglers may be to be sure to release fish at or near the site where you caught them so that you do not disrupt stable dominance hierarchies. Now that it is clear that living in a stable dominance hierarchy can be advantageous for a trout, it is fair to ask whether things might be even better for all concerned if that hierarchy were composed of relatives.

There is good reason to believe such might be the case. Current thinking has natural selection based on the relative number of copies of an animal's genes that are transmitted to the next generation. It is important to realize that an animal's relatives in the next generation (other than its own offspring) would bear such copies. For example, we can show theoretically that, all else being equal, an animal is better off behaving in a way that produces five nieces and nephews rather than two offspring. Selection for such traits that increase production of nonoffspring kin has been called *kinship selection* (Hamilton 1964), and the grounds are good for thinking such selection based on kin could function in salmonids.

Spawning trout or salmon lay numerous eggs in a depression that

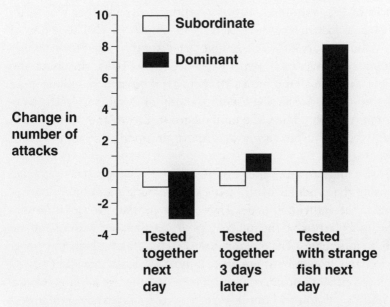

Figure 9.2. The Advantages of a Stable Dominance Hierarchy. Juvenile rainbow trout were housed in pairs until their dominant-subordinate relationship had been determined by observing their behavior. Then they were divided randomly into three groups of pairs. Pairs of fish in group 1 were kept together and tested the next day for their tendency to be aggressive toward each other. Pairs of fish in the second group were held apart for 3 days before being reunited for an aggression test. In group 3 the pairs were scrambled so that a subordinate fish from one pair was tested against a dominant fish from another pair.

The black and white bars at left show that when a pair of fish familiar with each other were retested the following day, they made fewer attacks on each other. After 3 days of separation the dominant (at least) seemed to have forgotten the former relationship to some extent because it increased its attack rate against the subordinate. However, fish rehoused with strangers clearly demonstrated the advantage of remaining in a stable dominance relationship. In that group the dominant used significantly more time and energy to re-establish its dominant status over a strange fish, even though the stranger had been subordinate in a former relationship, and of course the subordinate bore the brunt of the increased attack rate. (After Johnsson 1997)

is excavated within stream gravel. Because the eggs of a single laying female often are fertilized by more than one male, many young fish hatching together and growing up in the same area of a river are likely to be at least half-siblings. Is there any evidence that relatives recognize each other as such and behave in a way that increases each other's chances of survival (and eventual reproduction)? In other words, do they engage in behavior predicted by kinship theory? The young of some salmonids are known to be able to tell kin from nonkin on the basis of odor (Brown and Brown 1992). (See chapter 6 for the discussion of the idea that salmon return to their natal stream by following an odor trail to relatives living there.) A study of dominance-related behavior in Atlantic salmon and rainbow trout (Brown and Brown 1995) suggested that kinship can be an important modifier of the effects of dominance.

Brown and Brown created groups of brothers and sisters in the lab by raising the products of the artificial insemination of an individual female by an individual male. They raised another group, of nonkin young, after fertilizing the mixed eggs of four females with the mixed sperm of four males. The researchers tested the effects of kinship on aggression and growth by studying groups of 10 fish arranged in groups composed either of brothers and sisters or of same-age nonkin. Results for Atlantic salmon and rainbow trout were qualitatively similar, so I will concentrate only on the outcome for the trout.

The behavior of dominant fish toward subordinates in the group clearly demonstrated kinship selection. Brown and Brown classified as dominant the five faster-growing fish during the 2-week period of the experiment and considered to be subordinate the quintet growing more slowly. If the subordinate fish were their siblings, the dominants were less aggressive toward them than if they were not (figure 9.3a). Presumably because they could devote more attention to looking for food because of the decrease in aggression, subordinate kin trout foraged at a higher rate than subordinate nonkin (figure 9.3b). This nice study illustrates how kinship determines the value of a dominance-dependent mental process, attention to food, in a way predicted by natural selection.

Hunger State

Chapter 3 touches upon the physiology of hunger as an internal factor influencing trout thinking. Now let me detail some mechanisms for such a state-dependent influence by considering how hunger state can modify reactions to food and predators. I will conclude the chap-

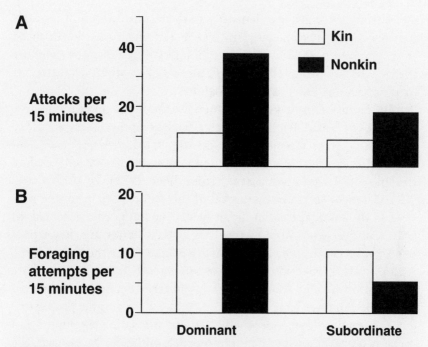

Figure 9.3. Family and Dominance in Rainbow Trout. Graph A shows that within groups of 10 brother-and-sister trout, dominant fish attacked subordinates less often than in groups of 10 nonkin trout. Presumably because they could reduce the amount of attention they paid to dominants, the subordinate brothers and sisters could feed at a higher rate than subordinate nonkin (graph B). Social dominants in the kin group also tended to forage more effectively than the dominants in the nonkin group, though such a trend could not be supported statistically. (After Brown and Brown 1995)

ter by considering the relative importance of dominance status and hunger state, because both must often exert their influences at the same time.

In a carefully controlled laboratory study Reiriz and colleagues (1998) fed individual Atlantic salmon parr from rivers in Spain and Scotland prey types encountered in their home rivers, specifically, a mayfly nymph, a trichopteran larva, and a scud. The researchers presented the three prey types one at a time in six replicates so that during its trial each fish would have the opportunity to take 18 prey items as they drifted by in the observation stream. Parr from both rivers always took the first several individuals of all three prey species, but by the end of the trial on average less than 50% of the test fish were still consuming prey. As they became sated, their reduced hunger clearly influenced their reaction to additional prey, although we cannot know whether the change was mediated though decreased perception, decreased attention, or some other aspect of cognition.

As I discussed in chapter 3, an animal is thought to monitor its state of hunger at least partially through stretch receptors in the digestive system. One project assumed that this stretch receptor response could be visualized as the amount of food present in the stomach divided by the amount of food present at satiation (Ware 1971). This study considered hunger to be the reciprocal of this value—the lower the proportion of maximal food in the stomach, the hungrier the animal. In Ware's project with rainbow trout the fish ate fewer and fewer prey items per second as their hunger state declined. Ware thought that the reason for this reduction in rate was an increase in handling time per item. Unfortunately, we do not know whether decreased hunger allowed the fish more time to maneuver the scud prey to the proper orientation for swallowing or whether hungry fish simply attempted and succeeded in swallowing scuds not oriented optimally. In any case, the animals' hunger state modified their decisions determining handling time to ingestion.

I have found little information of any kind about the reaction of trout to being hooked and released. With more anglers adopting the catch-and-release philosophy, a larger proportion of the fish in any system will experience this phenomenon. As a tool for taking into account fishing pressure in management decisions, it would be quite valuable to understand for how long after being caught a fish's thinking keeps it out of the catchable cohort. From the angler's perspective, it might be useful to understand to what extent a fish remembers and avoids the specific characteristics of a fly pattern associated by instrumental learning with the presumably negative reinforcement of being caught. One study of hook avoidance in rainbow trout (Yoneyama et al. 1996) found that the number of days of starvation influenced the extent of hook avoidance in previously caught rainbow trout.

Cases of anorexia show that under certain conditions, salmonids can ignore or perhaps not even mentally detect hunger, responses that drastically affect their reactions to food stimuli. Evidence of anorexia in both juvenile and adult Atlantic salmon exists. Young salmon parr maintain station in streams while feeding on drifting food. In the spring parr that have reached sufficient size transform into smolt and begin the downstream journey to the sea. However, some young fish of the same age do not reach the required size, and these small parr remain in the stream for another year before smolting. An experimental study in Scotland (Metcalfe and Thorpe 1992) demonstrated that whether overwintering parr became anorexic depended on their weight. For our purposes the project clearly showed that the altered state of hunger modified the fish's thinking about food.

From the autumn to the winter Metcalfe and Thorpe (1992) periodically tested young fish for their reaction to food pellets (figure 9.4). Because all the tested fish were small for their age, the control fish, which had gained weight in a normal fashion, ceased feeding by late November, even in the presence of superabundant food. By contrast, researchers starved fish in the experimental group for 3 weeks during early winter, resulting in loss of considerable fat. These salmon resumed feeding when given the opportunity in late November, by which time the controls had become anorexic. After the fish in the experimental group had made up the shortfall in body fat, they too entered a period of anorexia that lasted through the winter. As I mentioned in chapter 3, Metcalfe and Thorpe (1992) interpreted the anorexia to mean that during winter, when little food is available anyway, a fish not large enough to become a smolt the following spring would be better off if it avoided the predation risk attendant on actively feeding and instead remained quiet among the rocks at the bottom of a pool. Interestingly, fish large enough to smolt the following spring continued to actively feed and gain weight right through the winter. The interpretation here is that heavier smolts better survive the trip to the ocean, so if a fish is going to smolt and go, it should become as large as possible before doing so.

The interesting point is the changed reaction toward food at the onset of anorexia. Metcalfe and Thorpe (1992) tested parr individually for their reaction to food pellets drifted by one at a time. Each time a pellet came into a parr's range, the fish was awarded a point score of 0 to 6 for its reaction: 0 for no reaction, 1 for orienting toward the food, 2 for swimming toward the food but turning back before reaching it, 3

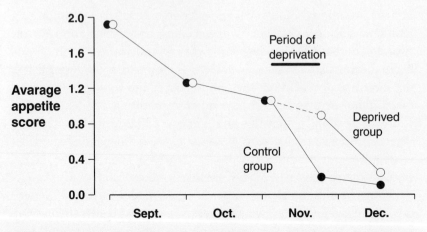

Figure 9.4. Anorexia in Juvenile Atlantic Salmon. As they approach winter, young salmon that will not migrate to the sea the following spring become anorexic; they cease feeding for the winter and remain dormant under stones in the riverbed. The graph shows that the fish's weight controls its anorexia and lack of response to food. When presented with drifting food pellets, juvenile salmon in an artificial stream were scored for their appetite, from 0 (no response) to 6 (ingestion). In the control group, which was fed a regimen of pellets throughout the period, appetites fell continually; by mid-November they had virtually stopped eating. In contrast, young fish deprived of all food for 3 weeks in November ate heartily when given the opportunity in late November, building up their body mass to the point where they again became anorexic by mid-December and joined the controls. (Metcalfe and Thorpe 1992)

for missing or rejecting the pellet, and 6 for eating it. The researchers calculated the average score for each fish in each group during each of four test periods.

The effect of the 3-week deprivation period on response to food was dramatic (figure 9.4). In the feeding trials immediately thereafter, the starved fish continued to respond to food, whereas the controls essentially ignored it. By the last feeding trial in mid-December the experimental fish had recovered the fat supply that they had lost during the fast, then became anorexic again.

Researchers have not yet figured out what change in mental processes caused the onset of indifference to food in the young salmon, but we have good evidence that the usual relationship between increased hunger and reaction to food did not apply.

At the other end of the life-history cycle of Atlantic salmon is another period of anorexia that the Scottish research group has also examined. As I noted earlier, in the discussion of physiological mechanisms of hunger, the onset of anorexia in maturing salmon was most closely associated with a threshold amount of lean body mass. Metcalfe and Thorpe (1992) provided no detailed records of the reaction to food, so we must be content to note that, once again, the onset of anorexia overrode normal influences of hunger on mental reactions.

Hunger or Rate Determination?

As I have shown, certain theories applied to the feeding behavior of trout have been based on such mathematical quantities as the ratios of energy to handling time and energy intake per unit of time. Cognitive ecologists are making a considerable effort to understand whether and how animals determine the rate at which things occur in their world (Shettleworth 1998). So far, experiments probing the abilities of animals to count things and measure small units of time, the two ingredients for calculating rates, have focused on birds and mammals. In researching this book, I found so little evidence for such an ability in trout or any other fish that I am not treating it separately. The problem is that an animal's hunger state often correlates with food intake rate, and we have good experimental evidence that hunger state can control many aspects of foraging behavior that might otherwise be attributed to counting and timing. Thus no one has needed to consider rate counting as an explanation for observed trout behavior. However, because one particular result with Dolly Varden char points to the possibility of rate counting that is independent of hunger state, and suggests a good system for further experimentation, it deserves mention.

Fausch and colleagues (1997) were investigating what threshold level of encountered prey might induce drift-feeding Dolly Varden char and Japanese white-spotted char to give up holding station at one point in a current in favor of moving about and probing for prey on the stream bottom. A nice feature was that the project was carried out with free-ranging fish in their natural habitat, an arrangement that reduced to a minimum the chances that some unsuspected aspect of the experiment would produce invalid results. After the researchers had noted prey capture rates of individually marked drift-feeding fish under unmanipulated conditions, they placed 1-mm-mesh screens upstream from the study pools. These screens vastly reduced the amount of invertebrate prey drifting down to the waiting char. Recall that in drift-feeding salmonids, the larger, more dominant individuals occupy the head of a pool and have first access to incoming food. Thus Fausch and colleagues predicted that the subordinate fish at the tail end of the chow line would be most affected by the reduction in food supply. As predicted, after they cut off the food supply (4.5 hours in one case, about 2.5 hours in another), subordinate Dolly Varden char gave up drift feeding and began to swim around the pool and forage for bottom-dwelling invertebrates. The authors calculated that such subordinate Dolly Vardens switched from drift feeding to bottom feeding when drift feeding alone brought them less than 15 prey items per 5-minute period (figure 9.5).

At first consideration it seems that the fish must have been using prey counts and time measurements to somehow calculate rate of prey capture. The difficulty with this idea comes when we realize that the authors lumped together the fish's feeding behavior during the entire period when drift was not present. Thus no one can rule out the possibility that the fish were simply reacting to a change of hunger state over several hours as the contents of their digestive tract were being processed without being replaced. What I would like to know is how fast the fish reacted to the change in capture rate. If it was within a minute or two of the change, for example, the fish could have processed little of their gut contents during such a brief interval, so I might be more willing to conclude that the fish could have been in some way comparing rates of capture. Although a minute-by-minute analysis was not germane to the purpose of the study, it would be quite interesting to have it done with the records now in hand. Incidentally, it was noteworthy that while the subordinate Dolly Vardens switched to bottom feeding, the subordinate white-spotted char did not. The authors ascribe the difference in response to the undershot lower jaw of the Dolly Varden, which probably makes bottom feeding more efficient for that species.

Although I have been discussing dominance and hunger as though they are independent mechanisms, some evidence demonstrates how these two state variables can interact to influence salmonid decisions. In a number of species of social animals, subordinate individuals begin

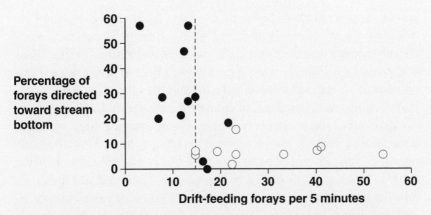

Figure 9.5. Why Dolly Varden Char Switch from Drift Feeding to Bottom Feeding. Wild fish in their native stream in Japan held station in the current and fed on drifting invertebrates. When researchers cut off the food supply by placing a fine-mesh screen upstream, subordinate fish switched to bottom feeding. Records suggested that the switch occurred whenever a fish made fewer than 15 forays after drifting prey items per 5-minute period. Each of the 11 fish in the study is represented twice in the figure, once for undisturbed conditions (open circles) and once for food-depleted conditions (closed circles). (After Fausch et al. 1997)

foraging first after a predator scare, which many researchers interpret as a decision by dominants to wait for the subordinates to demonstrate that the coast is clear before venturing from shelter. An experiment with the fabled Mirimichi River stock of Atlantic salmon suggests that hunger rather than dominance status directly determines who decides to leave shelter first after a predator attack (Gotceitas and Godin 1991). Gotceitas and Godin placed pairs of juvenile fish of equal length and weight in an aquarium together for 7 days during which they established a two-fish dominance hierarchy. After being transferred to a flow-through test tank, a pair was allowed to drift feed on brine shrimp before being "attacked" by a model belted kingfisher that researchers plunged into the tank. In every case the bird attack caused both fish to dart under the overhead cover provided in the test chamber. At the time of the attack the two fish were either equally hungry, meaning that one fish had eaten no more than three brine shrimp more than the other, or one of them was hungrier than the other (>4 shrimp difference in number of shrimp eaten). When the dominant was hungrier than the subordinate or when the two fish were equally hungry, the dominant fish was much more likely to be the first to leave shelter and presumably to risk predator attack while drift feeding in the open. By contrast, when the subordinate was the hungrier, it often left shelter and fed first. Thus it appeared that hunger state overrode any effect of dominance status on which fish decided to resume feeding in the open first. Under normal circumstances in nature, of course, dominants should be less hungry than subordinates because of their better foraging sites, so dominance status actually should determine hunger state. Similar results obtained from a number of species now can be viewed anew as being the result of hunger mediated by dominance status and not the direct result of dominance status. The subordinate takes the risk of the predator's still being around not because it is subordinate but because it is hungrier—but it is hungrier because it is subordinate.

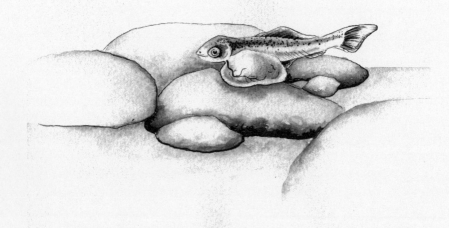

Chapter 10

Evolution and the Mind of the Trout

In the preceding chapters I have reviewed the evidence that trout, their allies, and other fishes think. These fish have the equipment to perceive light, mechanical stimuli, odor and taste molecules, and electromagnetism. Such internal factors as endogenous rhythms, hunger state, and hormone levels influence their responses to these environmental stimuli. Perception and attention partially dictate what trout react to in their surroundings. Learning and memory furnish stored information that the fish integrate with current sensory input to control their behavioral responses. Why has evolution furnished trout with the mental apparatus that they possess and not more or less?

Psychologists have traditionally been interested in the mechanisms of learning and memory. Much attention in the latter half of the twentieth century centered on comparing the prowess of various animal groups in common tests of "intelligence." M. E. Bitterman and his colleagues, leading proponents of this comparative approach, produced one study that compared the learning responses of laboratory rats and tilapia, a mouthbreeding fish native to the Great Lakes of East Africa. In one variant of the approach (1958) the Bitterman team awarded a food pellet to both rats and fish that pushed against a vertically or a horizontally striped target. The researchers varied the positions of the two targets between trials just to make sure the responses were not the result of an animal's preference for a target in one place or the other. After a rat or fish had performed at least 17 of 20 trials in a day without a mistake, the researchers switched the positions of the targets and rewarded the other one. Bitterman and colleagues were trying to determine how quickly a rat and a fish could learn about the switch. They concluded that the rat was able to learn to correct for reversals much more quickly than the fish could, a difference that the researchers attributed to the rat's having greater intelligence, or cognitive ability.

Evolutionary ecologists have a much different way of assessing comparative ability. We start by asking what is the average lifetime reproductive success per individual for any particular species? If we assume that in nature the population levels of both rats and fish are more or less stable, it follows that the average lifetime reproductive success per individual mammal and fish is about one. That is, on average, each animal contributes one offspring to the next generation. Using this criterion to assess cognitive ability, the unavoidable conclusion is that trout are just as cognitively competent in their environment as rats are in theirs. Pushing this line of reasoning to its logical conclusion, if we assume that population levels of tapeworms are also stable, tapeworms, which have no nervous system at all, must also have an average lifetime reproductive success of one and therefore must have a cognitive ability equal to that of rats and fish.

From an evolutionary perspective, asking about the comparative thinking ability of disparate species is not an interesting question. For example, salamanders, which have evolved from fish, have smaller, simpler brains than many present-day fish species (Roth et al. 1993; Striedter 1998). Does that mean that fish are more highly evolved than salamanders? What is interesting is to ask why any given species is not better or worse at thinking than it is—why has natural selection equipped animals of a species with just the type and extent of thinking ability that they now possess? The way to explore this question is through an optimality approach, which considers benefits and costs.

In general, across species, cognitive ability correlates positively with the amount of integrative tissue in the brain, a correlation culminating with the massive neocortex of humans. An important fact is that brain tissue is extremely expensive to maintain metabolically. For example, in humans a given amount of brain tissue requires twenty-two times as much energy to maintain as a similar amount of muscle tissue (Aiello 1997). Put another way, a human must eat twenty-two times more food to support metabolically a cubic centimeter of brain than a cubic centimeter of muscle. A major theme of this book has been that natural selection should favor any sort of attribute that augments lifetime reproductive success. From this perspective any increase in cognitive ability clearly must be highly adaptive if natural selection is to favor it despite the tremendous cost of the additional neural tissue required. All else being equal, we expect natural selection always to favor the metabolically least expensive mechanism of behavioral control. Thus the range of control mechanisms, from simple reflex to genetically fixed innate response to learning and memory, may form a graded series of metabolic cost.

If the environmental stimuli causing a response are simple, relatively intense, and important for survival and reproduction, we might expect natural selection to favor reflexive responses because of the low cost of the neural mechanism required. The startle response to a diving predator is an example of such a reflex.

At a more complicated level are the innate or genetically programmed responses to sign stimuli. The alarm reaction to the odor of trout skin is a good example. A second example is provided by the genetically programmed response to current by juvenile sockeye salmon (Raleigh 1967).

Soon after hatching, young sockeye move from their birth site in a stream to a nearby lake where they spend the first year or two of life before continuing on to the ocean. Sockeye spawn in both inlet and outlet streams of some lakes. Young fish from inlet streams innately swim with the current, which brings them to the lake. Conversely, those young fish hatching in outlet streams innately swim against the current, a response that also gets them to the lake. The intense selection against any inlet or outlet youngster's swimming the wrong way has maintained these two genetically determined responses in the apparent absence of cognition. An interesting follow-up to this story has capitalized on the finding that some sockeye have recently taken to spawning in Lake Washington itself rather than in inlet or outlet streams (Hensleigh and Hendry 1998). The researchers had expected that because young hatched in the lake would not be under intense selective pressure to move either with or against a current, such responses might have been lost or diminished. However, the lake fish turned out to swim even more strongly with the current than fish from a nearby inlet stream. The researchers concluded that the response of the lake-spawned fish occurred as a result of random change in their genetic composition in the absence of natural selection and that because there was no selection for or against movement in a current, the lake fish could have just as easily evolved to swim against, rather than with, a current in an artificial test set-up such as Hensleigh and Hendry used.

Odor imprinting is another form of information gathering that appears to be simpler than cognition based on conventional forms of learning. Imprinting could be considered a form of cognition because it includes acquisition and storage of information for later recall. However, because imprinting occurs only once during an innately determined short period in a young fish's life and appears never to be forgotten, the neural underpinnings of this imprinting may be less extensive than those of more complex forms of cognition.

As we imagine responses that require more and more metabolically costly brain tissue, the next level might involve pairing by learning a response of high fitness value to an innate response. In the parlance of classical conditioning, if the conditioned stimulus is simple in nature and if the conditioned response is of great value for reproductive success, such learning may be selected to be rapid and long lasting. The learning of an alarm response to pike odor, paired with the odor of trout skin, seems to be a good example of such a simple form of cognition. In Brown and Smith's study (1998) we saw that such learning occurred after only one trial.

Instrumental learning seems to have the most potential for capitalizing on an extensive brain. We have an intuitive familiarity with such learning by experience. We save learned items in our memory, then recall them later, often in combination with other memories. Because big brains are expensive, attempts have been made to relate increased cognitive ability with particular environments. Let us now explore this matter with fish other than salmonids and hope that future studies along similar lines use trout and their relatives.

As there are about 25,000 species of fish, occurring in virtually all aquatic habitats, several researchers have attempted to correlate brain development with different types of environment. The thinking is that if one compares closely related species, say, those in the same taxonomic family, the variation in brain structure must be the result of divergent evolution. That is, differences among closely related species must have occurred as the group branched off new species in a variety of habitat types.

In considering the increase in size and importance of various parts of the brain, we might wonder whether such growth through evolutionary time could have been limited by the size of the cranium, or braincase. This question leads to the interesting discovery that, unlike what we find in other groups of vertebrates, the braincase of fish is much larger than the brain. In fact, a fish brain is suspended in and surrounded on all sides by a thick layer of fatty tissue. Why is this? Could it be that the fat provides insulation and that the brain of a trout, which generates twenty-two times more metabolic heat than muscle, is therefore kept warmer than the rest of the body? If this is true, how does it relate to the issue of temperature-specific learning and memory that I raised earlier? Anyway, braincase size has apparently not been a constraint on the evolution of larger brain components in fish.

One study of African mouthbreeding fish concluded that development of different sensory centers of the brain is associated with divergent types of feeding behavior and predator avoidance (Kotrschal et al. 1998). In species inhabiting open water, particularly at great depth, where there is little light and little acoustical noise, the lateral line system and associated areas of the brain are well developed. Among bottom feeders, brain centers for smell and taste become prominent. Clear water has favored development of large retinas and large image-processing areas in the brain. Finally, there is a correlation between shallow-water habitats complex in structure (reeds, rock formations) and species with particularly large forebrains, the location of information integration and storage in fish. Kotrschal and colleagues thought that this correlation reflects the increased selection for processing and storage of complex flows of information from vision. Although their review concluded with a call for testing whether habitat-specific anatomies, particularly of forebrain development, are related to variation in cognitive ability, other researchers had already started to work along these lines with sticklebacks.

In Scotland three-spined sticklebacks live in both rivers and ponds. Could it be that sticklebacks living in ponds, where landmarks might be relatively stable in time and space, might be inclined to use landmarks as a learning aid in a test situation? By contrast, might riverine sticklebacks, living in a situation with less visibility because of water turbulence and where strong currents during spates might periodically modify landmarks, be less likely to use landmarks in a learning task? Girvan and Braithwaite (1998) addressed these questions by allowing fish from both habitats to learn to negotiate a maze to a food source. The maze consisted of a series of barriers, each containing one door to the remainder of the maze and one false door leading to a dead end. In some trials with each type of fish, researchers placed a small water plant as a landmark next to each of the doors leading to food. (A companion experiment showed conclusively that the fish could not have been finding the food by its odor alone.)

In a comparison of maze swimming in the presence and absence of the water-plant landmarks, fish from the two habitats showed markedly different behavior. The presence of the plants markedly increased the performance level of the pond fish but had no influence on the performance of river fish (figure 10.1). Girvan and Braithwaite (1998) interpreted these results as supporting the notion that the population of pond sticklebacks was somehow influenced by its habitat to use landmarks in the maze but the river fish were not. The researchers suggested that river fish instead might have learned and remembered the correct series of left-right decisions that led to the food.

The same researchers next explored whether the difference in landmark use between the two sorts of sticklebacks could have had a genetic basis or whether it was due to upbringings in two very different habitats. In a somewhat more complicated design, they allowed sticklebacks to to grow up from the fry stage under three different regimes. For 10 months "pond-stable" fish grew up in a tank with six plastic plant landmarks kept in constant position. Girvan and Braithwaite allowed "pond-unstable" fish to grow up during the same period in a tank in which the positions of six similar landmarks were varied five times per week. "River-pond" young were the progeny of river-caught adults but were allowed to grow for 10 months in a pond.

As before, Girvan and Braithwaite trained fish in the maze with and without the water plant landmarks next to "correct" doors. In this experiment, however, the test came when the positions of the correct door (accompanied by the water-plant landmark) and the incorrect

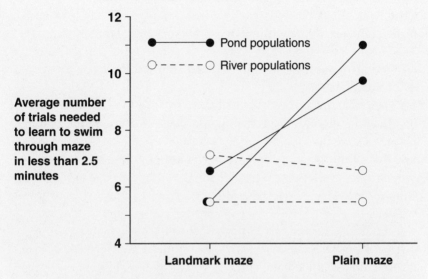

Figure 10.1. Environmental Influences on Learning. Pond and riverine sticklebacks showed significant differences in their ability to learn maze-swimming cues. If each correct turn in the maze was marked by a water-plant landmark, two sets of pond fish learned the maze faster than if landmarks were missing. By contrast, landmarks had no effect on the maze learning of fish from two riverine populations. Researchers interpreted these responses as reflecting the increased opportunity for pond fish to navigate using learned landmarks. (After Girvan and Braithwaite 1998)

door were reversed at each barrier. If fish were using the landmarks, they should quickly switch doors, but if they were using some other learning method, such as remembering the sequence of correct doors, they should switch more slowly.

At first exposure to the reversed maze, fish from all three groups immediately followed the landmarks, making no mistakes even when the researchers had switched correct and incorrect door at each barrier. Thus it appeared from this result that no genetically determined differences govern the learning of river and pond sticklebacks. Also, within pond sticklebacks the tendency to learn and use landmarks in the maze was not related to whether a fish had grown up among stable or unstable landmarks.

A second stickleback study (Mackney and Hughes 1995) addressed the issue of memory, testing the notion that fish from a more stable environment might have better memories for learned details than fish from more variable environments. Mackney and Hughes compared 15-spined sticklebacks from a marine population for their memory of a foraging technique with three-spined sticklebacks from an estuary and from a freshwater site.

The researchers maintained all three sorts of fish in captivity for 2 months on a diet of mysid shrimp and then presented them with amphipods (scuds) as food during trials for the next 10 days. As noted earlier, these little crustaceans have backward-pointing bristly legs, and fish learn to swallow them head first. After 10 days fish from all three habitats had learned to handle and eat the scuds as quickly as they ever would.

The critical test of memory came when the sticklebacks were again given scuds after various intervals. Estuarine and marine sticklebacks showed almost immediately that they had begun to forget how to handle the bristly crustaceans (figure 10.2), at rates averaging 13% and 18% per day, respectively. By contrast, even after a lapse of 25 days, the freshwater fish caught and ate scuds as rapidly as ever; they had forgotten nothing about the technique.

These results lead to the interesting idea that forgetting might be adaptive. Mackney and Hughes suggested that freshwater pond sticklebacks live in quite a stable environment, where the complex of potential prey species is not likely to change rapidly. In estuarine and marine habitats the array of prey should be more variable as the tides rise and fall. Also, individual fish in saltwater habitats are likely to move around more than their freshwater counterparts. The possibility therefore exists that forgetting a technique useful for one prey type may be an adaptation to a changing environment because remembering it might interfere with processing a different type of food item. Whether these differences have a genetic basis or were the result of the different environments in which the fish grew up could be examined with animals from the three habitat types reared from eggs under similar conditions. The experiment used only two species of stickleback, so it's possible that some of the difference in response could have been due to different species' histories. However, this explanation is less likely to hold for the contrast between estuarine and pond fish, because they were of the same species.

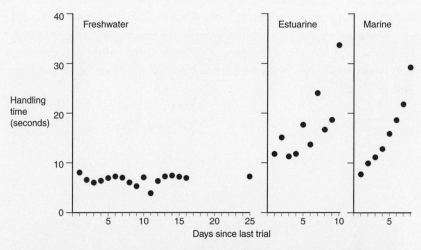

Figure 10.2. Environment and Memory Loss in Sticklebacks. Sticklebacks from a fresh-water pond remembered quite well how to handle and eat scuds efficiently, showing no increase in handling time per scud even after a hiatus of 25 days. By contrast, stickle-backs from an estuary forgot efficient handling methods at an average rate of about 13% per day. For marine sticklebacks the memory loss was even more rapid, about 18% per day. These results were related to the possibility that more variable food supplies in estuarine and marine waters might select for more rapid loss of memory of how to handle any given food type. (After Mackney and Hughes 1995)

A final point about adaptive brain size and cognitive function is that parts of the brain may grow and recede through time in much the same way that other organs of the body do. For example, the ovaries and testes of birds change greatly in size between breeding and nonbreeding seasons. Researchers believe that when the reproductive organs are not functioning, natural selection has favored their reduction in size so they cost less energy to maintain and to carry in flight against the force of gravity.

Other groups of animals have provided good evidence that brain components grow and recede throughout the year as their functioning becomes more or less important to survival and reproduction. Clayton (1995) has shown that certain birds that cache food for later use have phenomenal memories for the location of individually cached items. This study also showed that such caching is accompanied by a rapid increase in the size of the hippocampus, a portion of the brain concerned with spatial memory. In seasons when caching does not occur, the hippocampus reverts to a smaller size. This sort of waxing and waning of brain parts is just what we would expect, given the very high cost of maintaining brain tissue. Students of salmonid cognition may want to search for correlates between the dynamics of thinking and brain anatomy.

Appendix 1

Experimental Angling

Although suggestions abound for what artificial lures an angler should use under what conditions, few or none of these claims are based on experimental records. Most seem to be somewhere between witchcraft and snake oil. But, then, those promoting the use of one fly or another are often attempting to catch anglers, not trout. My intention in this appendix is to place angling on a scientific footing by describing in detail a method for determining, objectively, whether one fly or lure is better than another. Many of the studies that I have discussed use the same general scientific method.

As in all experiments, we begin with a hypothesis. For example, suppose we think that the size of a fly might be important in inducing a trout to strike. (Recall from chapter 5 that specific search image suggests that food item size might be an important cue for feeding fish.) By rewording this question, we arrive at what is known as an *alternative hypothesis,* namely, that the size of a fly influences the tendency of a trout to strike. We also create a so-called null hypothesis, in this case that fly size has no influence on strike tendency. As is the case with all hypotheses, these statements are too general to test universally; we cannot test all artificial flies and all trout. Therefore, from the hypothesis we deduce one or more predictions that we can test directly. In formal language we say that if the hypothesis is true—that fly size is an important characteristic in inducing a strike—the prediction must also be true that trout in certain streams tend to strike with different frequency at large and small deer-hair caddis dry flies. Similarly, if the null hypothesis is true, strike frequency should be unrelated to the size of the caddis imitation.

The next step in the scientific method is to test the prediction. In this case a proper test should control for any factor other than fly size that might confound the response of a trout. We might go about testing our prediction in the following manner. (These suggestions are for an ideal test. In the real world we must often make do with less than the ideal while still learning something worthwhile.) Two investigators work as a team. They begin by securing two identical sets of rod, reel, line, and leader. They use these two outfits on a number of different stretches of water, never fishing any stretch more than once. (Such a restriction is necessary so that no fish is exposed to the test arrangement more than once.) Each day the investigators toss a coin to determine who on that day is designated as the angler and who is the assistant (or gillie, if the test is to be conducted in the British Isles). As determined by coin toss, the larger caddis, say, a #12, is tied to the leader of one rod and the smaller, say, a #18, to the leader of the other. Then, by coin toss, the angler selects one rod for the first cast. As the two investigators work their way along the stream, the angler and assistant exchange rods after every cast, so that the angler is alternating presentation of the large and small flies. (If alternating with this frequency seems onerous, they could trade rods after every five casts or some other arbitrary number.)

We are interested in the number of casts of each fly that results in strikes. Each day the investigators tally the numbers of both casts and strikes for each fly. Thus the two workers might decide to build up records of their trials on 20 different days on 20 different stretches of water. The only necessity for the analysis that I describe shortly is that the aggregate number of casts over all days must be the same for the two sizes of fly. (Equal numbers of casts of large and small flies are not a requirement, but if they are not equal, the analysis becomes more complicated.) The null hypothesis predicts that the fish will strike equally often at the large and smaller flies if the number of casts from each are equal. By contrast, the alternative hypothesis says that more casts of either the larger or smaller fly should produce strikes. Note that the alternative hypothesis does not predict which fly should provoke more strikes, only that one or the other will.

An entire way of life (some call it a subculture) is devoted to statistical analysis. Such analyses are an agreed-upon method for determining whether an alternative hypothesis is false. The present case hinges on whether two quantities are different or not, and we will use a statistical test called the Chi-square test to find out. If the null hypothesis of no difference is correct, we should expect equal numbers of strikes at the larger and smaller caddis. Suppose that 41 of 800 casts with the larger fly provoked strikes and 22 of 800 with the smaller did so. The question is, could this difference have happened purely by chance, or was there really a difference in the trout's tendency to strike at the larger and smaller offering? Suppose the trout were completely indifferent to fly size. In a large number of trials we would expect about equal numbers of strikes at large and small flies. In the present case we garnered 63 total strikes. If the trout had no preference, we would expect these 63 strikes to be divided into 31.5 strikes at each size fly. (Note that even though there are no partial real casts, the calculation can result in partial expected casts.) Although the details of statistics are beyond the scope of this book, let me note here that the Chi-square test tells us that the likelihood is less than 5% that the results we obtained could have been due solely to chance. How are we to interpret the results of such a test? You found that trout struck more at the larger or smaller offering, so the prediction deduced from the alternative hypothesis is true. What about the hypothesis itself? You have failed to disprove the alternative hypothesis, but you have not proved it to be true. For all we know, the difference may apply only to deer-hair caddis. In general, we can prove a prediction true or false, but we can never prove a hypothesis to be true; we can only fail to disprove it.

One remarkable and little appreciated attribute of science is that we can never prove anything to be true; we can only fail to show that it is false. In practice we build our confidence in a hypothesis by testing many different predictions deduced from it and always finding that the predictions are true. In the present case, if we were to test the size hypothesis across dozens of fly types and dozens of streams and always found a size difference in strikes provoked, we would begin to believe the hypothesis, even though we could never prove it true. Ultimately, science is a belief system.

The objective, controlled approach to angling can be used to answer a large number of questions. Does hackle color matter? Does time of day matter? Is one stream more productive than another? Do brook trout strike more readily than brown trout? Does the color of the bead on bead-head pheasant-tail nymphs matter? Is one angler more skilled than another?

This last question about angler competence could be examined automatically if, in the set of tests I have described, the two investigators switched roles of angler and assistant each time they worked a new stretch of water. In practice the question is whether they differ in the proportion of their casts that produced strikes regardless of the size of the fly. Note that we have a complication here if they use wet flies, because the two anglers may not be equal in their ability to determine whether they actually have a strike. Perhaps this last question is best studied with dry flies, where both investigators can agree on whether a strike occurs.

Appendix 2

Scientific Names of Species
Mentioned in Text

Bee, honey	*Apis mellifera*
Burbot	*Lota lota*
Caterpillar, woollybear	*Platyprepia virginalis*
Char	*Salvelinus*
Arctic	*Salvelinus alpinus*
Dolly Varden	*Salvelinus malma*
white-spotted	*Salvelinus leucomaenis*
Chicken	*Gallus gallus*
Chub, lake	*Couesius plumbeus*
Cod	*Gadus morhua*
Daphnia	*Daphnia* sp.
Eagle	*Haliaeetus leucocephalus*
Goldfish	*Carassius auratus*
Grayling, Arctic	*Thymallus arcticus*
Grizzly	*Ursus arctos*
Guppy	*Poecilia reticulata*
Jay, blue	*Cyanocitta cristata*
Kingfisher, belted	*Ceryle alcyon*
Mealworm	*Tenebrio molitor*
Merganser, common	*Mergus merganser*
Osprey	*Pandion haliaetus*

Pigeon	*Columba livia*
Pickerel	*Esox niger*
Pike, northern	*Esox lucius*
Rat, Norway	*Rattus norvegicus*
Salmon, Atlantic	*Salmo salar*
chinook	*Oncorhynchus tshawytscha*
chum	*Oncorhynchus keta*
coho	*Oncorhynchus kisutch*
sockeye	*Oncorhyncus nerka*
Scud	*Gammarus* sp.
Stickleback, fifteen-spined	*Spinachia spinachia*
three-spined	*Gasterosteus aculeatus*
Sunfish, bluegill	*Lepomis macrochirus*
Swordtail	*Xiphophorus helleri*
Tilapia	*Tilapia macrocephala*
Topminnow	*Aplocheilus lineatus*
Trout, Apache	*Oncorhynchus apache*
brook	*Salvelinus fontinalis*
brown	*Salmo trutta*
cutthroat	*Oncorhynchus clarki*
Gila	*Oncorhynchus gilae*
rainbow	*Oncorhynchus mykiss*
redband	*Oncorhynchus mykiss gairdneri*
steelhead	*Oncorhynchus mykiss*
Tuna, albacore	*Thunnus albacares*
Whitefish	*Coregonus pallasi*

References

Abbott, J. C., R. L. Dunbrack, and C. D. Orr. 1985. The interaction between size and experience in dominance relationships of juvenile steelhead trout (*Salmo gairdneri*). *Behaviour* 92:241 53.

Adron, J. W., P. T. Grant, and C. B. Cowey. 1973. A system for the quantitative study of the learning capacity of rainbow trout and its application to the study of food preferences and behaviour. *Journal of Fish Biology* 5:625–36.

Aiello, L. C. 1997. Brains and guts in human evolution: the expensive tissue hypothesis. *Brazilian Journal of Genetics* 20:141–48.

Allan, J. D. 1981. Determinants of diet of brook trout (*Salvelinus fontinalis*) in a mountain stream. *Canadian Journal of Fisheries and Aquatic Science* 38:184–92.

Anderson, N. H. 1966. Depressant effect of moonlight on activity of aquatic insects. *Nature* 209:319–20.

Andrew, R. J. 1985. The temporal structure of memory formation. *Perspectives in Ethology* 6:219–59.

Angradi, T. R. 1992. Effects of predation risk on foraging behavior of juvenile rainbow trout (*Oncorhynchus mykiss*). *Canadian Journal of Zoology* 70:355–60.

Bader, R. B. 1997. A functional classification of the drift: traits that influence invertebrate availability to salmonids. *Canadian Journal of Fisheries and Aquatic Sciences* 54:1211–34.

Baggerman, B. 1960. Salinity preference, thyroid activity, and the seaward migration of four species of Pacific salmon (*Oncorhynchus*). *Journal of Fisheries Research Board of Canada* 17:295–322.

Bamford, O. S. 1974. Oxygen reception in the rainbow trout (*Salmo gaird-neri*). *Comparative Biochemistry and Physiology* 48A:69–76.

Bannon, E., and N. H. Ringler. 1986. Optimal prey size for stream resident brown trout (*Salmo trutta*): tests of predictive models. *Canadian Journal of Zoology* 64:704–13.

Bardach, J. E., and R. C. Bjorklund. 1957. Temperature sensitivity of some American freshwater fish. *American Naturalist* 91:233–52.

Barrett, J. C., G. D. Grossman, and J. Rosenfeld. 1992. Turbidity-induced changes in reactive distance of rainbow trout. *Transactions of the American Fisheries Society* 121:437–43.

Beamish, F. W. H. 1980. Swimming performance and oxygen consumption of the charrs. Pp. 739–48 in *Charrs, salmonid fishes of the genus* Salvelinus. E. K. Balon (ed.). Junk, The Hague, Netherlands.

Beaudet, L., I. N. Flamarique, and C. W. Hawryshyn. 1997. Cone receptor topography in the retina of sexually mature Pacific salmonid fishes. *Journal of Comparative Neurology* 393:49–59.

Behnke, R. J. 1991. "Warmwater" trout. P. 131 in *Trout.* J. Stoltz and J. Schnell (eds). Stackpole Books, Harrisburg, Pa.

Bitterman, M. E., J. Wodinsky, and D. K. Candland. 1958. Some comparative psychology. *American Journal of Psychology* 71:94–109.

Blair, G. R., D. E. Rogers, and T. P. Quinn. 1993. Variation in life history characteristics and morphology of sockeye salmon (*Oncorhynchus nerka*) in the Kvichak River system, Bristol Bay, Alaska. *Transactions of the American Fisheries Society* 122:550–59.

Bleckmann, H. 1988. Prey identification and prey localization in surface feeding fish and fishing spiders. Pp. 619–41 in *Sensory biology of aquatic animals.* J. Atema, R. R. Fay, A. N. Popper, and W. N. Tavolga (eds.). Springer, New York.

Bleckmann, H. 1993. Role of the lateral line in fish behaviour. Pp. 201–46 in *Behaviour of teleost fishes.* T. J. Pitcher (ed). Chapman and Hall, London.

Bleckmann, H., G. Tittel, and E. Gronau-Blubaum. 1989. The lateral line system of surface-feeding fish: anatomy, physiology, and behavior. Pp. 501–26 in *The mechanosensory lateral line: neurobiology and evolution.* S. Coombs, P. Gorner, and H. Munz (eds.). Springer, New York.

Blough, P. M. 1989. Attentional priming and visual search in pigeons. *Journal of Experimental Psychology: animal Behavior Processes* 15:358–65.

Bone, Q., N. B. Marschall, and J. H. S. Baxter. 1995. *Biology of fishes.* 2d ed. Blackie Academic and Professional, London.

Bowmaker, J. K., and Y. W. Kunz. 1987. Ultraviolet receptors, tetrachromatic colour vision, and retinal mosaics in the brown trout (*Salmo trutta*): age-dependent changes. *Vision Research* 27:2101–8.

Braithwaite, V. A., J. D. Armstrong, H. M. McAdam, and F. A. Huntingford. 1996. Can juvenile Atlantic salmon use multiple cue systems in spatial learning? *Animal Behaviour* 51:1409–15.

Brand, J. G., and R. C. Bruch. 1992. Molecular mechanisms of chemosensory transduction: gustation and olfaction. Pp. 126–49 in *Fish chemoreception*. T. J. Hara (ed.). Chapman and Hall, London.

Brett, J. R., and N. R. Glass. 1973. Metabolic rates and critical swimming speeds of sockeye salmon (*Oncorhynchus nerka*) in relation to size and temperature. *Journal of the Fisheries Research Board of Canada* 30:379–87.

Browman, H. I., I. Novales-Falamarique, and C. W. Hawryshyn. 1994. Ultraviolet photoreception contributes to prey search behaviour in two species of zooplanktivorous fishes. *Journal of Experimental Biology* 186:18–98.

Brown, G. E., and J. A. Brown. 1992. Do rainbow trout and Atlantic salmon discriminate kin? *Canadian Journal of Zoology* 70:1636–40.

Brown, G. E., and J. A. Brown. 1995. Does kin-based territorial behavior increase kin-based foraging in juvenile salmonids? *Behavioral Ecology* 7:24–29.

Brown, G. E., and R. J. F. Smith. 1998. Acquired predator recognition in juvenile rainbow trout (*Oncorhynchus mykiss*): conditioning hatchery-reared fish to recognize chemical cues of a predator. *Canadian Journal of Fisheries and Aquatic Science* 55:611–17.

Bryan, J. E., and P. A. Larkin. 1972. Food specialization by individual trout *Journal of the Fisheries Research Board of Canada* 29:1615–24.

Bulwalda, R. J. A., A. Schuijf, and A. D. Hawkins. 1983. Discrimination by the cod of sounds from opposing directions. *Journal of Comparative Physiology* 150:175–84.

Butler, R. L. 1991. Rogue trout. P. 81 in *Trout*. J. Stoltz and J. Schnell (eds.). Stackpole Books, Harrisburg, Pa.

Charnov, E. 1976. Optimal foraging: attack strategy of a mantid. *American Naturalist* 110:141–51.

Chew, G. L., and G. E. Brown. 1989. Orientation of rainbow trout (*Salmo gairdneri*) in normal and null magnetic fields. *Canadian Journal of Zoology* 67:641–43.

Chivers, D. P., and R. J. F. Smith. 1994. Fathead minnows, *Pimephales promelas*, acquire predator recognition when alarm substance is associated with the sight of unfamiliar fish. *Animal Behaviour* 48:597–605.

Clarke, G. L. 1954. *Elements of ecology.* John Wiley and Sons, New York.

Clayton, N. S. 1995. Development of memory and the hippocampus: comparison of food-storing and nonstoring birds on a one-trial associative memory task. *Journal of Neuroscience* 15:2796–807.

Cleveland, L., E. E. Little, C. G. Ingersoll, R. H. Wiedmeyer, and J. B. Hunn. 1991. Sensitivity of brook trout to low pH, low calcium, and elevated aluminum concentrations during laboratory pulse exposures. *Aquatic Toxicology* 19:303–18.

Contor, C. R., and J. S. Griffith. 1995. Noctural emergence of juvenile rainbow trout from winter concealment relative to light intensity. *Hydrobiologica* 299:179–83.

Covert, J. B., and W. W. Reynolds. 1977. Survival value of fever in fish. *Nature* 267:43–45.

Croy, M. I., and R. N. Hughes. 1991. The role of learning and memory in the feeding behaviour of the fifteen-spined stickleback, *Spinachia spinachia* L. *Animal Behaviour* 41:149–59.

Cuenca, E. M., and M. Delahiguera. 1994. Evidence for an endogenous circadian-rhythm of feeding in the trout (*Oncorhynchus mykiss*). *Biological Rhythm Research* 25:228–35.

Davson, H. 1964. *General physiology.* Little, Brown, Boston.

Dill, L. M. 1987. Animal decision making and its ecological consequences: the future of aquatic ecology and behaviour. *Canadian Journal of Zoology* 65:803–11.

Dill, L. M., and A. H. G. Fraser. 1984. Risk of predation and the feeding behavior of juvenile coho salmon (*Oncorhynchus kisutch*). *Behavioral Ecology and Sociobiology* 16:65–71.

Dittman, A. H., and T. P. Quinn. 1996. Homing in Pacific salmon: mechanisms and ecological basis. *Journal of Experimental Biology* 199:83–91.

Dittman, A. H., T. P. Quinn, and G. A. Nevitt. 1996. Timing of imprinting to natural and artificial odors by coho salmon (*Oncorhynchus kisutch*). *Canadian Journal of Fisheries and Aquatic Sciences* 53:434–42.

Douglas, P. L., G. E. Forrester, and S. C. Cooper. 1994. Effects of trout on the diel periodicity of drifting baetid mayflies. *Oecologia* 98:48–56.

Douglas, R. H. 1990. Goldfish use the visual angle of a familiar landmark to locate a food source. *Journal of Fish Biology* 49:532–36.

Douglas, R. H., and C. W. Hawryshyn. 1990. Behavioural studies of fish vision: an analysis of visual capabilities. Pp. 373–418 in *The visual system of fish.* R. H. Douglas and M. B. A. Djamgoz (eds.). Chapman and Hall, London.

Døving, K. B., H. Nordeng, and B. Oakley. 1975. Single unit discrimination of fish odours released by char (*Salmo alpinus*) populations. *Comparative Biochemical Physiology* 47A:1051–63.

Dull, C. E., H. C. Metcalfe, and J. E. Williams. 1960. *Modern physics*. Holt, New York.

Edmundson, E., F. E. Everest, and D. W. Chapman. 1968. Permanence of station in juvenile chinook salmon and steelhead trout. *Journal of the Fisheries Research Board of Canada* 25:1453–64.

Elliot, J. M. 1976. The energetics of feeding, metabolism, and growth of brown trout (*Salmo trutta* L.) in relation to body weight, water temperature, and ration size. *Journal of Animal Ecology* 45:923–48.

Elliot, J. M. 1991. Tolerance and resistance to thermal stress in juvenile Atlantic salmon, *Salmo salar*. *Freshwater Biology* 25:61–70.

Elliot, J. M. 1994. *Quantitative ecology and the brown trout*. Oxford University Press, Oxford.

Eriksson, L.-O., and H. Lundqvist. 1982. Circannual rhythms and photoperiod regulation of growth and smolting in Baltic salmon (*Salmo salar* L.). *Aquaculture* 28:113–21.

Eriksson, L. -O., H. Lundqvist, E. Brannas, and T. Eriksson. 1982. Annual periodicity of activity and migration in the Baltic salmon, *Salmo salar* L. Pp. 415–30 in *Coastal research in the Gulf of Bothnia*. K. Muller (ed.). Junk, The Hague, Netherlands.

Eriksson, T. 1984. Adjustments in annual cycles of swimming behaviour in juvenile Baltic salmon in fresh and brackish water. *Transactions of the American Fisheries Society* 113:467–71.

Essington, T. E., and P. W. Sorensen. 1996. Overlapping sensitivities of brook and brown trout to putative hormonal pheromones. *Journal of Fisheries Biology* 48:1027–29.

Evans, D. H. 1998. *The physiology of fishes*. 2d ed. CRC Press, Boca Raton, Fla.

Facey, D. E., and G. D. Grossman. 1990. The metabolic cost of maintaining position for four North American stream fishes: effects of season and velocity. *Physiological Zoology* 63:757–76.

Fausch, K. D., N. Shigeru, and S. Kitano. 1997. Experimentally induced foraging mode shift by sympatric charrs in a Japanese mountain stream. *Behavioral Ecology* 8:414–20.

Fernald, R. D. 1990. The optical system of fishes. Pp. 45–61 in *The visual system of fish*. R. H. Douglas and M. B. A. Djamgoz (eds.). Chapman and Hall, London.

Gerkema, M. P. 1992. Biological rhythms: mechanisms and adaptive values. Pp. 27–37 in *Rhythms in fishes*. M. A. Ali (ed.). Plenum Press, New York.

Gern, W. A., S. S. Greenhouse, J. M. Nervina, and P. J. Gasser. 1992. The rainbow trout pineal organ: an endocrine photometer. Pp. 199–218 in *Rhythms in fishes*. M. A. Ali (ed.). Plenum Press, New York.

Gilliam, J. F., and D. F. Fraser. 1987. Habitat selection under predation hazard: test of a model with foraging minnows. *Ecology* 68:1856–62.

Gilmour, K. M. 1998. Gas exchange. Pp. 101–27 in *The physiology of fishes*. D. H. Evans. (ed.). CRC Press, Boca Raton, Fla.

Girvan, J. R., and V. A. Braithwaite. 1998. Population differences in spatial learning in three-spined sticklebacks. *Proceedings of the Royal Society of London* B 265:913–18.

Godin, J.-G. J., and S. A,. Smith. 1988. A fitness cost of foraging in the guppy. *Nature* 333:69–71.

Gotceitas, V., and J.-G. J. Godin. 1991. Foraging under risk of predation in juvenile Atlantic salmon (*Salmo salar* L.)—Effects of social status and hunger. *Behavioral Ecology and Sociobiology* 29:255–61.

Gould, J. L. 1982. *Ethology: the mechanisms and evolution of behavior*. W. W. Norton, New York.

Gowan, C., M. K. Young, K. D. Fausch, and S. C. Riley. 1994. Restricted movement in resident stream salmonids: a paradigm lost? *Canadian Journal of Fisheries and Aquatic Science* 51:2626–37.

Greenberg, L. A., E. Bergman, and A. G. Eklöv. 1997. Effects of predation and intraspecific interactions on habitat use and foraging by brown trout in artificial streams. *Ecology of Freshwater Fish* 6:16–26.

Gries, G., K. G. Whalen, F. Juanes, and D. L. Parrish. 1997. Nocturnal activity of juvenile Atlantic salmon (*Salmo salar*) in late summer: evidence of diel activity partitioning. *Canadian Journal of Fisheries and Aquatic Sciences* 54:1408–13.

Grove, D. J., L. G. Loizides, and J. Nott. 1978. Satiation amount, frequency of feeding, and gastric emptying rate in *Salmo gairdneri*. *Journal of Fisheries Biology* 12:507–16.

Halvorsen, M., and O. B. Stabell. 1990. Homing behaviour of displaced stream-dwelling brown trout. *Animal Behaviour* 39:1089–97.

Hamilton, W. D. 1964. The genetical evolution of social behaviour. *Journal of Theoretical Biology* 7:1–52.

Hara, T. J. 1993. Role of olfaction in fish behaviour. Pp. 172–99 in *Behaviour of teleost fishes*. 2d ed. T. J. Pitcher (ed.). Chapman and Hall, London.

Hara, T. J. 1994. Olfaction and gustation in fish: a review. *Acta Physiologica Scandinavica* 152:207–17.

Hasler, A. D., and A. T. Scholz. 1983. *Olfactory imprinting and homing in salmon: investigations into the mechanisms of the imprinting process.* Springer-Verlag, Berlin.

Hawkins, A. D. 1993. Underwater sound and fish behaviour. Pp. 129–69 in *Behaviour of teleost fishes.* T. J. Pitcher (ed.). Chapman and Hall, London.

Hawkins, A. D., and A. D. F. Johnstone. 1973. The hearing of the Atlantic salmon, *Salmo salar. Journal of Fish Biology* 13:655–73.

Hawryshyn, C. W., M. G. Arnold, E. Bowering, and R. L. Cole. 1990. Spatial orientation of rainbow trout to plane-polarized light: the ontogeny of e-vector discrimination and spectral sensitivity characteristics. *Journal of Comparative Physiology* A:565–74.

Hawryshyn, C. W., and F. I. Hárosi. 1994. Spectral characteristics of visual pigments in rainbow trout (*Oncorhynchus mykiss*). *Vision Research* 34:1385–92.

Hawryshyn, C. W., and W. N. McFarland. 1987. Cone photoreceptor mechanisms and the detection of polarized light in fish. *Journal of Comparative Physiology* A 160:459–65.

Heggenes, J., O. M. W. Krog, O. R. Lindås, J. G. Dokk, and T. Bremnes. 1993. Homeostatic behavioural responses in a changing environment: brown trout (*Salmo trutta*) become nocturnal during winter. *Journal of Animal Ecology* 62:295–308.

Heiligenberg, W. 1974. Processes governing behavioural states of readiness. *Advances in the Study of Behaviour* 5:173–200.

Henderson, M. A. 1982. An analysis of prey detection in cutthroat trout (*Salmo clarki clarki*) and Dolly Varden charr (*Salvelinus malma*). Unpublished Ph.D. diss., University of British Columbia.

Hensleigh, J. E., and A. P. Hendry. 1998. Rheotactic response of fry from beach-spawning populations of sockeye salmon: evolution after selection is relaxed. *Canadian Journal of Zoology* 76:2186–93.

Hess, E. H. 1973. *Imprinting.* Van Nostrand, New York.

Hill, J., and G. D. Grossman. 1993. An energetic model of microhabitat use for rainbow trout and rosyside dace. *Ecology* 74:685–98.

Holmgren, S., D. J. Grove, and D. J. Fletcher. 1983. Digestion and the control of gastrointestinal motility. Pp. 23–40 in *Control processes in fish physiology.* J. C. Rankin, T. J. Pitcher, and R. T. Duggan (eds.). Croom Helm, London.

Horvath, G., and D. Varju. 1995. Underwater refraction-polarization patterns of skylight perceived by aquatic animals through Snell's window of the flat water surface. *Vision Research* 35:1651–66.

Hughes, N. F. 1992a. Ranking of feeding positions by drift-feeding Arctic grayling (*Thymallus arcticus*) in dominance hierarchies. *Canadian Journal of Fisheries and Aquatic Sciences* 49:1994–98.

Hughes, N. F. 1992b. Selection of positions by drift-feeding salmonids in dominance hierarchies: model and test for Arctic grayling (*Thymallus arcticus*) in subarctic mountain streams, interior Alaska. *Canadian Journal of Fisheries and Aquatic Sciences* 49:1999–2008.

Hughes, N. F. 1998. A model of habitat selection by drift-feeding stream salmonids at different scales. *Ecology* 79:281–94.

Hughes, R. N. 1979. Optimal diets under the energy maximization premise: the effects of recognition time and learning. *American Naturalist* 113:209–21.

Hughes, R. N., M. J. Kaiser, P. A. Mackney, and K. Warburton. 1992. Optimizing foraging behaviour through learning. *Journal of Fish Biology* 41 (Supplement B):77–91.

Huntingford, F. A. 1984. *The study of animal behaviour.* Chapman and Hall, London.

Huntingford, F. A., N. B. Metcalfe, and J. E. Thorpe. 1993. Social status and feeding in Atlantic salmon *Salmo salar* parr: the effect of visual exposure to a dominant. *Ethology* 94:201–6.

Jacobs, G. H. 1992. Ultraviolet vision in vertebrates. *American Zoologist* 32:544–54.

Johnson, L. 1966. Experimental determination of food consumption of pike, *Esox lucius,* for growth and maintenance. *Journal of Fisheries Research Board of Canada* 23:1495–1505.

Johnsson, J. I. 1997. Individual recognition affects aggression and dominance relations in rainbow trout (*Oncorhynchus mykiss*). *Ethology* 103:267–82.

Johnsson, J. I., and M. V. Abrahams. 1991. Interbreeding with domestic strain increases foraging under threat of predation in juvenile steelhead trout (*Oncorhynchus mykiss*): an experimental study. *Canadian Journal of Fisheries and Aquatic Science* 48:243–47.

Kadri, S., N. B. Metcalfe, F. A. Huntingford, and J. E. Thorpe. 1995. What controls the onset of anorexia in maturing adult female Atlantic salmon? *Functional Ecology* 9:790–97.

Kadri, S., J. E. Thorpe, and N. B. Metcalfe. 1997. Anorexia in one-sea-winter Atlantic salmon during summer, associated with sexual maturation. *Aquaculture* 151:405–9.

Karlsen, H. E., and O. Sand. 1987. Selective and reversible blocking of the lateral line in fishes. *Journal of Experimental Biology* 133:249–62.

Keefe, M. L., and H. E. Winn. 1991. Chemosensory attraction to home stream water and conspecifics by native brook trout, *Salvelinus fontinalis*, from two southern New England streams. *Canadian Journal of Fisheries and Aquatic Sciences* 48:938–44.

Knudsen, F. R., C. B. Schreck, S. M. Knapp, P. S. Enger, and O. Sand. 1997. Infrasound produces flight and avoidance responses in Pacific juvenile salmonids. *Journal of Fish Biology.* 51:824–29.

Kotrschal, K., M. J. Van Staaden, and R. Huber. 1998. Fish brains: evolution and environmental relationships. *Reviews in Fish Biology and Fisheries* 8:373–408.

Krebs, J. R. 1977. The significance of song repertoires: the Beau Geste hypothesis. *Animal Behaviour* 25:475–78.

Laland, K. N., and K. Williams. 1997. Shoaling generates social learning of foraging information in guppies. *Animal Behaviour* 53:1161–69.

Lauf, R. F., and C. H. Wood. 1996. Respiratory gas exchange, nitrogenous waste excretion, and fuel usage during aerobic swimming in juvenile rainbow trout. *Journal of Comparative Physiology* B 166:501–9.

Lee, R. M., and J. N. Rinne. 1980. Critical thermal maxima of five trout species in the southwestern United States. *Transactions of the American Fisheries Society* 109:632–35.

Ligo, M., H. Kezuka, K. Aida, and L. Hanyu. 1991. Circadian rhythms of melatonin secretion from superfused goldfish (*Carassius auratus*) pineal glands *in vitro*. *General Comparative Endocrinology* 83:152–58.

Lloyd, J. E. 1965. Aggressive mimicry in *Photuris:* firefly femmes fatales. *Science* 149:653–54.

Loew, E. R., and W. N. McFarland. 1990. The underwater visual environment. Pp. 1–43 in *The visual system of fish*. R. H. Douglas and M. B. A. Djamgoz (eds.). Chapman and Hall, London.

Love, R. M. 1970. *The chemical biology of fish*. Vol. 1. Academic Press, London.

McIntosh, A. R., and B. L. Peckarsky. 1996. Differential behavioural responses of mayflies from streams with and without fish to trout odor. *Freshwater Biology* 35:141–48.

Mackney, P. A., and R. N. Hughes. 1995. Foraging behaviour and memory window in sticklebacks. *Behaviour* 132:1241–53.

Mann, S., N. H. C. Sparks, M. M. Walker, and J. L. Kirschvink. 1988. Ultrastructure, morphology, and organization of biogenic magnetite from sockeye salmon, *Oncorhynchus nerka:* implications for magnetoreception. *Journal of Experimental Biology* 140:35–49.

Manning, A., and M. S. Dawkins. 1998. *An introduction to animal behaviour*. Cambridge, Cambridge University Press.

Martel, G., and L. M. Dill. 1993. Feeding and aggressive behaviors in juvenile coho salmon (*Oncorhynchus kisutch*) under chemical-mediated risk of predation. *Behavioral Ecology and Sociobiology* 32:365–70.

Martel, G., and L. M. Dill. 1995. Influence of movement by coho salmon (*Oncorhynchus kisutch*) parr on their detection by common mergansers (*Mergus merganser*). *Ethology* 99:139–49.

Meddis, R. 1975. On the function of sleep. *Animal Behaviour* 23:676–91.

Menzel, R., U. Greggers, and M. Hammer. 1993. Functional organization of appetitive learning and memory in a generalist pollinator, the honey bee. Pp. 79–125 in *Insect learning: ecological and evolutionary perspectives*. D. Papai and A. Lewis (eds.). Chapman and Hall, London.

Metcalfe, N. B., and J. E. Thorpe. 1992. Anorexia and defended energy levels in overwintering juvenile salmon. *Journal of Animal Ecology* 61:175–81.

Metcalfe, N. B., S. K. Valdimarsson, and N. H. C. Fraser. 1997. Habitat profitability and choice in a sit-and-wait predator: juvenile salmon prefer slower currents on darker nights. *Journal of Animal Ecology* 66:866–75.

Milinski, M. 1994. Long-term memory for food patches and implications for ideal free distributions in sticklebacks. *Ecology* 75:1150–56.

Mirza, R. S., and D. P. Chivers. 2000. Predator-recognition training enhances survival of brook trout: evidence from laboratory and field-enclosure studies. *Canadian Journal of Zoology* 78:2198–2208.

Moran, D. T., J. C. Rowley, G. R. Aiken, and B. W. Jafek. 1992. Ultrastructural neurobiology of the olfactory mucosa of the brown trout, *Salmo trutta*. *Microscopy Research and Technique* 23:28–48.

Moulton, J. M., and R. H. Dixon. 1967. Directional hearing in fishes. Pp. 187–232 in *Marine bio-acoustics*. Vol. 2. W. N. Tavolga (ed.). Pergamon Press, Oxford, U.K.

Moyle, P. B. 1969. Comparative behavior of young brook trout of domestic and wild origin. *Progressive Fish-Culturist* 31:51–59.

Nair, I., M. G. Morgan, and H. K. Florig. 1989. *Biological effects of power frequency electric and magnetic fields*. Background paper, OTA-BPO-E-53. U.S. Government Printing Office, Washington, D.C.

Nielsen, J. L., T. E. Lisle, and V. Osaki. 1994. Thermally stratified pools and their use by steelhead in Northern California streams. *Transactions of the American Fisheries Society* 123:613–26.

O'Brien, W. J., and J. J. Showalter. 1993. Effects of current velocity and suspended debris on the drift feeding of Arctic grayling. *Transactions of the American Fisheries Society* 122:609–15.

Peter, R. E. 1979. The brain and feeding behavior. Pp. 121–59 in *Fish physiology*. W. S. Hoar, D. J. Randall, and J. R. Brett (eds.). Academic Press, New York.

Pietrewicz, A. T., and A. C. Kamil. 1981. Search images and the detection of cryptic prey: an operant approach. Pp. 311–31 in *Foraging behavior: ecological, ethological, and psychological approaches*. A. C. Kamil and T. D. (eds.). Sargent Garland STPM Press, New York.

Quinn, T. P., R. T. Merrill, and E. L. Brannon. 1981. Magnetic field detection in sockeye salmon. *Journal of Experimental Zoology* 217:137–42.

Rahmann, H., G. Jeserich, and I. Zeutzius. 1979. Ontogeny of visual acuity of rainbow trout under normal conditions and light deprivation. *Behaviour* 68:315–22.

Raleigh, R. F. 1967. Genetic control in the lakeward migrations of sockeye salmon (*Oncorhynchus nerka*). *Journal of the Fisheries Research Board of Canada* 24:2613–22.

Rask, M., P. J. Vuorinen, J. Raitaniemi, A. Lappalainen, and S. Peuranen. 1992. Whitefish stocking in acidified lakes—ecological and physiological responses. *Hydrobiologica* 243:277–82.

Reebs, S. 1992. Sleep, inactivity, and circadian rhythms in fish. Pp. 127–35 in *Rhythms in fishes*. Plenum Press, New York.

Reiriz, L., A. G. Nicieza, and F. Brana. 1998. Prey selection by experienced and naive juvenile Atlantic salmon. *Journal of Fish Biology* 53:100–114.

Richards, J. A., Jr., F. W. Sears, M. R. Wehr, and M. W. Zemansky. 1960. *Modern university physics*. Addison-Wesley, Reading, Mass.

Rincón, P. A., and J. Lobón-Cerviá. 1993. Microhabitat use by stream-resident brown trout: bioenergetic consequences. *Transactions of the American Fisheries Society* 122:575–87.

Ringler, N. H. 1979. Selective predation by drift-feeding brown trout (*Salmo trutta*). *Journal of the Fisheries Research Board of Canada* 36:392–403.

Ringler, N. H. 1985. Individual and temporal variation in prey switching by brown trout, *Salmon trutta*. *Copeia* 1985:918–26.

Roberts, J. L. 1973. Effects of thermal stress on gill ventilation and heart rate in fishes. Pp. 64–86 in *Responses of fish to environmental changes*. W. Chavin (ed.). Charles C. Thomas, Springfield, Ill.

Robinson, F. W., and J. C. Tash. 1979. Feeding by Arizona trout (*Salmo apache*) and brown trout (*Salmo trutta*) at different light intensities. *Environmental Biology of Fishes* 4:363–68.

Roth, G., K. C. Nishikawa, C. Naujoksmanteuffel, A. Schmidt, and D. B. Wake. 1993. Pedomorphosis and simplification in the nervous-system of salamanders. *Brain, Behavior, and Evolution* 42:137–70.

Sánchez-Vázquez, F. J., and M. Tabata. 1998. Circadian rhythms of demand feeding and locomotor activity in rainbow trout. *Journal of Fish Biology* 52:255–67.

Schellart, N. A. M. and R. J. Wubbels. 1998. The auditory and mechanosensory lateral line system. Pp. 283–312 in *The physiology of fishes*. 2d ed. D. H. Evans (ed.). CRC Press, Boca Raton, Fla.

Schmitz, M. 1992. Annual variations in rheotactic behaviour and seawater adaptability in landlocked Arctic char (*Salvelinus alpinus*). *Canadian Journal of Fisheries and Aquatic Science* 49:448–52.

Schuijf, A., and A. D. Hawkins. 1983. Acoustic distance discrimination by the cod. *Nature* 302:143–44.

Shettleworth, S. J. 1998. *Cognition, evolution, and behavior*. Oxford University Press, New York.

Shezifi, Y., E. Kimmel, and A. Diamant. 1997. The electrophysiological response of fish to hypoxia. *Aquacultural Engineering* 16:253–59.

Shields, W. H. 1982. *Philopatry, inbreeding, and the evolution of sex*. State University of New York Press, Albany.

Smith, J. J., and H. W. Li. 1983. Energetic factors influencing foraging tactics of juvenile steelhead trout, *Salmo gairdneri*. Pp. 173–80 in *Predators and prey in fishes*. D. L. G. Noakes, D. G. Lindquist, G. S. Helfman and J. A. Ward (eds.). Junk, The Hague, Netherlands.

Sorensen, P. W., and J. Caprio. 1998. Chemoreception. Pp. 375–405 in *The physiology of fishes*. 2d ed. D. H. Evans (ed.). CRC Press, Boca Raton, Fla.

Striedter, G. F. 1998. Progress in the study of brain evolution: from speculative theories to testable hypotheses. *Anatomical Record* 253:105–12.

Sundström, L. F., and J. I. Johnsson. 2001. Experience and social environment influence the ability of young brown trout to forage on live normal prey. *Animal Behaviour* 61:249–55.

Sutterlin, A. M., and S. Waddy. 1975. Possible role of the posterior lateral line in obstacle entrainment by brook trout (*Salvelinus fontinalis*). *Journal of the Fisheries Research Board of Canada* 32:2441–46.

Swain, D. P., and B. E. Riddell. 1990. Variations in agonistic behaviour between newly emerged juveniles from hatchery and wild populations of coho salmon, *Oncorhynchus kisutch*). *Canadian Journal of Fisheries and Aquatic Science* 47:566–71.

Thorpe, W. H. 1963. *Learning and instinct in animals*. 2d ed. Harvard University Press, Cambridge, Mass.

Tinbergen, L. 1960. The natural control of insects in pinewoods, I: Factors influencing the intensity of predation by song birds. *Archives Neerlandaises de Zoologie* 13:265–343.

Tolman, E. C. 1948. Cognitive maps in rats and men. *Psychological Review* 55:189–208.

Tolman, E. C., and C. H. Honzik. 1930. Introduction and removal of reward, and maze performance in rats. *University of California Publications in Psychology* 4:257–75.

Valentincic, T., and J. Caprio. 1997. Visual and chemical release of feeding behavior in adult rainbow trout. *Chemical Senses* 22:375–382.

Valone, T. J. 1996. Food-associated calls as public information about patch quality. *Oikos* 77:153–57.

Vinyard, G. L., and W. J. O'Brien. 1976. Effects of light and turbidity on the reactive distance of the bluegill sunfish (*Lepomis macrochirus*). *Journal of the Fisheries Research Board of Canada* 33:2845–49.

Wagner, E. J., and T. Bosakowski. 1994. Performance and behaviour of rainbow trout reared in covered raceways. *Progressive Fish Culturist* 56:123–29.

Walker, M. M., C. E. Diebel, C. V. Haugh, P. M. Pankhurst, J. C. Montgomery, and C. R. Green. 1997. Structure and function of the vertebrate magnetic sense. *Nature* 390:371–76.

Wang, L., and R. J. White. 1994. Competition between wild brown trout and hatchery greenback cutthroat trout of largely wild parentage. *North American Journal of Fisheries Management* 14:475–87.

Warburton, K. 1990. The use of local landmarks by foraging goldfish. *Animal Behaviour* 40:500–505.

Ware, D. M. 1971. Predation by rainbow trout (*Salmo gairdneri*): the effect of experience. *Journal of the Fisheries Research Board of Canada* 28:1847–52.

Wiley, R. H. 1983. The evolution of communication: information and manipulation. Pp. 156–89 in *Animal Behaviour*. Vol. 2: *Communication*. T. R. Halliday and P. J. B. Slater (eds.). Blackwell Scientific Publications, Oxford, U.K.

Wiley, R. H. 1994. Errors, exaggeration, and deception in animal communication. Pp. 157–89 in *Behavioral mechanisms in evolutionary ecology*. L. A. Real (ed.). University of Chicago Press, Chicago.

Wunder, W. 1927. Sinnesphysiologische Untersuchungen über die Nahrungsaufnahme bei verschiedenen Knochenfischarten. *Zeitschrift vergleichen Physiologie* 6:67–98 (cited by Bleckmann 1993).

Yoneyama, K., T. Matsuoka, and G. Kawamura. 1996. The effect of starvation on individual catchability and hook-avoidance learning in rainbow trout. *Bulletin of the Japanese Society of Scientific Fisheries* 62:236–42 (Japanese with English summary).

Young, M. K. 1996. Summer movements and habitat use by Colorado River cutthroat trout (*Oncorhynchus clarki pleuriticus*) in small, montane streams. *Canadian Journal of Fisheries and Aquatic Science* 53:1403–8.

Young, M. K., R. A. Wilkison, J. M. Phelps, and J. S. Griffith. 1997. Contrasting movement and activity of large brown trout and rainbow trout in Silver Creek, Idaho. *Great Basin Naturalist* 57:238–44.

Zaunreiter, M., R. Brandstatter, and A. Goldschmid. 1998. Evidence for an endogenous clock in the retina of rainbow trout, I: Retinomoter movements, dopamine, and melatonin. *Neuroreport* 9:1205–9.

Subject Index

Attention, 91; attractor patterns, 92; competitors and, 104; distractor, 91; dominance and, 105; pop-out effect, 92; predation risk and, 100; specific search image, 96; target, 92

Beau Geste hypothesis, 78
Biological rhythms: circannual, 42; circadian, 45; endogenous, 41

Causation of behavior: proximate, 117; ultimate, 117
Char, Arctic: circannual rhythm, 44; habitat imprinting, 129; salinity, response to, 37
Char, brook: drifting invertebrates, effect on, 87; lateral line, 23; pop-out effect, 92; temperature, response to, 3
Char, Dolly Varden: light intensity, effect of, 82; rate determination, possibility of, 155
Chemical senses. See Smell; Taste
Cognitive behavior, 3; evolution of, 161; —, habitat effects, 165; state-dependent, 145 —, dominance, 145; —, hunger, 150
Cognitive maps, 139

Drift, of food items, 86

Energy. See Metabolism
Experimental angling, 171
Eye, 11

Fitness: definition, 3; relative, 125

Goldfish: cognitive map, 140; temperature, 34
Grayling, Arctic: debris in drift, response to, 83; habitat selection, 60; metabolism, 60
Guppy: attention, divided, effect of, 100; social learning, 131

Habituation. See Learning
Hormones, 9
Hunger state, 52

Imprinting. See Learning

Learning: classical conditioning, 120; habituation, 109; imprinting, 127; —, habitat, 128; —, sexual, 128; —, social, 128; instrumental, 112; latent, 126; operant, 112; social, local enhancement, 130; social facilitation, 130; temperature-dependent, 134
Light: attenuation of, 9, 11; diffraction of, 10; polarized, 11; ultraviolet, 11

Magnetic sense, 28
Mechanical perception; definition, 18; inner ear, 18; —, lateral line, 21; —, surface waves, 23
Memory: food patches, 135; food types, 134; handling techniques, 135; temperature and, 137

191

Author Index